HARPER & ROW, PUBLISHERS

YORK, EVANSTON, AND LONDON

THE RES

NEW

THE RESCUER

BY PETER MAAS

FIRST EDITION

LIBRARY OF CONGRESS CATALOG CARD NUMBER: 67–23048

H-R

This is for Audrey

CONTENTS

THE RESCUER

1

AT HALF PAST SEVEN O'CLOCK IN THE MORNING ON MAY 23, 1939, the submarine *Squalus* slipped seaward from a rock-bound cove at the mouth of the Piscataqua River, a twisting tidal millrace which divides Maine and New Hampshire as it spills into the North Atlantic. The *Squalus* had been out on maneuvers the day before as well, so her skipper, Lieutenant Oliver Naquin, remained downstream overnight instead of returning to his home base at the Portsmouth Navy Yard farther up the river. Knowing this, Naquin's pretty brunette wife, Frances, decided to give their two children a special treat. In the late afternoon she had driven down from Portsmouth with them to the cove where the *Squalus* stretched low in the water behind an ocean breakwater. But by the time they arrived it had started raining and in the gloomy twilight nobody came on deck to answer their shouts and waves. Mrs. Naquin often thought of this during the terrible hours that lay ahead.

The specter of these same hours had—for more than fourteen years—driven a man in relentless and perilous preparation for them. His name was Charles Bowers Momsen and at that time he was a lieutenant commander in the U.S. Navy stationed in Washington, D.C. For most people the worth of their lives in the end is a mixture of grays, to be measured on balance. But for Momsen, this Tuesday in May, the judgment would come swiftly and in black and white.

Swede Momsen was forty-three. He had picked up the nickname at Annapolis, although his ancestry was North German and Danish. He was just six feet tall; he had an unruly thatch of light brown hair, a square jaw and a soft-spoken, reflective manner. He would have looked at home on the bridge of a Scandinavian tramp steamer. Beneath his composed exterior he was, in fact, an extraordinary combination of visionary, scientist and man of action. By the time he hung up his hat, many would say he was the greatest submariner the Navy ever had. But above all else, he was a human being.

As usual, Momsen was up at six o'clock and in the kitchen of his home on the outskirts of Washington brewing the first of the countless cups of coffee he downed during a day. He used the quiet of these early hours to collect his thoughts and to review the ideas that were constantly occurring to him. He had plenty on his mind. During the past twenty months he had been heading up an experimental diving unit at the Washington Navy Yard. And under his leadership a major breakthrough had been achieved. In a highly complex series of tests he had shown that careful mixtures of helium and oxygen, instead of air, enabled a diver to operate efficiently at depths far beyond three hundred feet, then the accepted working limit beneath the surface.

The going was treacherous, however. Time and again, in proving out theory, a diver in the Navy yard's big pressure tank would be hit by the bends, the crippling bubbles that can form in the bloodstream after exposure to great pressure. A particularly harrowing experience had taken place a few days before. As pressure in the tank was lowered to simulate an ascent from the ocean floor, the diver inside suddenly crumpled. To everybody watching through the thick glass eyeports it looked like another case of the bends. The normal thing would have been to raise the pressure in the tank quickly again and reduce it more gradually. Momsen was ready to give the order when some instinct held him back. All he had to go on was an apparently minor point: the stricken diver failed to complain about the sharp pain that usually accompanied an actual attack. So, while his assistants gaped in amazement, Momsen directed the pressure in the tank to be dropped completely, the unconscious man hauled out and rushed to a nearby recompression chamber. Later, samples of air taken from the tank turned out to be loaded with deadly carbon monoxide; it had come from burning lubricants in the tank's air compressors. If the pressure within the tank had been raised, the diver's life would have been snuffed out instantly. As it was, he barely pulled through.

By chance, on May 23rd, Momsen's first thoughts centered on the Portsmouth Navy Yard. His winter tests under controlled laboratory conditions were practically over. It was time now to try them in the ocean itself. In early June, Momsen planned to take his diving team up to Portsmouth and work out of there for the rest of the summer. A good deal of material had already been sent and more was due to be shipped that day. He spent the better part of an hour on a letter to Portsmouth officials detailing the care and storage of his equipment until he arrived.

Then he went back upstairs with coffee and juice for his wife, Anne. She had been bedded down with a bad cold and he promised he would try to get home early that afternoon. Outside, it was hot and muggy. It was going to be the first really uncomfortable day of the season in Washington. So Momsen left wearing a panama hat and a cotton suit. He climbed into the two-year-old Packard sedan he had bought new in Shanghai before being returned to duty in the U.S. As he drove along the Potomac toward the Navy yard, he consoled himself with visions of the cool weather he would be enjoying next month off the New England coast.

There, some six hundred miles to the northeast, the *Squalus*, a big white "192" painted on each side of her conning tower, cleared the Piscataqua River and churned into the North Atlantic once more. She was the Navy's newest fleet-type submarine, 310 feet long, 1,450 tons. Her name was Latin; it meant a shark. She had been built at the Portsmouth Navy Yard, launched there the previous September and commissioned in March. On board she carried five officers, fifty-one crewmen and three civilian technicians who were assisting in her shakedown tests. Three weeks hence she was scheduled to undergo formal sea trials before joining the operational fleet.

Today she was to run through one of these trials. It would be her eighteenth dive. Her first submergence, to make sure she was watertight, had taken place in early April while she was still in her berth at Portsmouth. The first tentative dip beneath the surface under her own power—her deck and superstructure not yet completed—was on April 20th in Portsmouth Harbor. After surfacing, one of her main motor bearings developed trouble; it was a relatively minor matter to remedy.

All construction work on the *Squalus* was finally finished on May 12th and three days later she began full-scale training at sea. The first order of business was to get her dives down pat. In wartime it could mean the difference between her life and death.

In one type of dive she rode with her ballast tanks high and dry. This allowed her to travel at top surface speed—some sixteen knots. But from here she had to complete an emergency battle descent that would drop her to periscope depth—fifty feet— within sixty seconds. It was to work on this dive that the *Squalus* now headed into the Atlantic.

A few days earlier, on May 17th, she had missed her target time in a similar exercise by less than five seconds. Lieutenant Naquin hoped she would do even better this trip. The *Squalus* was Naquin's second command. He had come out of Annapolis in 1925 and, at thirty-five, had six years in submarine service behind him. He was a precise, somewhat humorless man with a hawk-like nose and frosty blue eyes which rarely changed expression.

By May 23rd Naquin was quite pleased with the way things had been going on board the *Squalus*. The crew seemed to be meshing together nicely and the "boat" herself was performing beautifully.* He had been particularly impressed by the manner in which she handled at slow speeds underwater during dummy torpedo firings. To top everything off he had received a congratulatory "well done" from Rear Admiral Cyrus Cole, the Commandant at Portsmouth. Now, as Naquin stood up on the bridge, he saw the early morning sun fade behind a bank of gray clouds scudding across the sky. The wind freshened and began to kick up a nasty chop that shot plumes of white foam over her rolling bow. Off to his right, a couple of lobstermen were already beating their way back to port. It would be a good day, Oliver Naquin thought, not to be on the surface.

Naquin's satisfaction that morning was shared by Harold Preble, a civilian naval architect on board. Preble's job was to see to it that the *Squalus* performed mechanically up to par during her test runs. For almost twenty-two years he had been doing this sort of thing in every submarine out of Portsmouth. And although it wasn't in his province, he privately noted how well the crew's

---

* In the Navy submarines are called boats, not ships.

training had progressed. Preble also considered the *Squalus* to be the finest submarine he had ever been in. He even rated her better than the *Sculpin,* her sister ship, which she had followed down the ways.

For the Navy the *Squalus* was the last word in submarine design. Seemingly, every care and precaution had been lavished on her; she was up-to-date, safe—and deadly. Such efforts were paying off. Certainly few flaws had turned up thus far. After her first submergence at dockside, the big thirty-one-inch main induction valve in her conning tower* had failed to open properly; through it air was fed to her diesel engines when the *Squalus* ran on the surface. The whole valve assembly had been taken apart as a result, put together again and had since worked perfectly. There was also the bearing trouble during her second dive. Then, yesterday, an electrical wire leading from a torpedo tube to its recording gear for performance data had malfunctioned. So that was the sum of it—a stuck valve, a hot bearing and a loose wire. Preble couldn't recall another instance of less difficulty in a new submarine. Except for faster reloading of her torpedo tubes—and a little more practice would take care of this—he figured that the *Squalus* was ready to pass her sea trials.

Her crew was as pleased. Like those in other submarines in the fleet, most of the men were experienced petty officers. In the *Squalus,* the ratio was even higher than usual; fully 90 per cent were able to sport the twin silver dolphins marking them as qualified submariners. They had started reporting for duty long before the *Squalus* was completed, and as they watched her take shape, they became acquainted with every facet of her delicate innards. The tricky business of running her demanded nothing

---

* I use "conning tower" as it is popularly thought of—the entire superstructure that rises above a submarine's main deck. Technically, it is a compartment inside this superstructure. I have used laymen's terms rather than technical ones throughout the book wherever possible.

less; a single slip in any of the hundreds of steps involving her daily routine could transform her instantly from a sleek underseas prowler into a tomb for them all.

For a twenty-year-old seaman named John Marino it was a time of high adventure. Marino wanted to get a rating as a torpedoman. A small-town boy from central Iowa, he was one of the lucky few newly selected for underseas duty. The *Squalus* was his first submarine. It was going to be his last.

Even for a veteran electrician's mate like John Batick the *Squalus* was a revelation. She was faster and more maneuverable than anything he had ever been on board before. Most important, he found her unbelievably spacious. Batick, the sleeves of his denim shirt rolled high to exhibit a Red Cross nurse tattooed on one arm and a gypsy girl on the other, never ceased to be amazed that he could drink a cup of coffee in the crew's mess without jamming his elbow in somebody's teeth.

Anyone except a submariner would have called Batick crazy. With the incredible array of paraphernalia packed inside her hull, the *Squalus* seemed more like a claustrophobic nightmare. But by previous standards she was spacious. All told, she was divided into seven major compartments, each of which could be closed off from the others by watertight doors.

Up front, in the bow, was her forward torpedo room.

The forward battery was next. Naquin's minuscule stateroom was there, as well as quarters for the other commissioned officers and chief petty officers on board. The compartment's name came, however, from the storage batteries housed in the space below deck that supplied the *Squalus* with her underwater power. Half the big batteries she carried with her were down there. To reach them you had to squeeze through a hatch set in the passageway just outside Naquin's room.

Behind the forward battery—and squarely under the conning

tower—was the control room. Down here her two periscopes came to rest. And jammed into a cabin twenty-one by nineteen feet were all the elements that made her tick—her internal communications center, the wheels that moved her diving planes up or down, the levers that flooded her ballast tanks and emptied them again. Here, too, was the control board that showed whether she was sealed against the sea before she slid beneath the surface.

The other half of her underwater power source was in the after battery where most of the crew slept and all of it ate. In front were thirty bunks in stacks of three; next came the galley and mess tables. The whole compartment, in which John Batick luxuriated, was less than forty feet long. In between the sleeping and eating areas a deck hatch led to the batteries below. Batick was going to have to crawl down among them this morning. Following the dive, Lieutenant Naquin intended to push the *Squalus* at her maximum rate beneath the surface for one hour and Batick's thankless task was to observe how the batteries operated under such stress.

Directly behind the after battery—in the forward engine room —the deep throb of two of her surface diesels beat steadily, wisps of brownish smoke from their exhausts trailing over the water outside her hull. Behind it, in the after engine room, were two more diesels and the electric motors that turned over her propellers. When the *Squalus* submerged, these motors, now working in tandem with her diesels, would be hooked up instead to the twin battery groups.

In her tail she carried a lethal wallop. Besides the four torpedo tubes in her bow, she had four more in the after torpedo room— for firing TNT warheads at anything that might lie astern of her. As up forward, the big snub-nosed torpedoes were ranged in racks three high; a system of pulleys swung them into position.

Torpedoman First Class Sherman Shirley would be stationed there for the morning dive this May 23rd. As he started back, he

paused briefly to chat in his Arkansas twang with his good friend
Lloyd Maness. The following Sunday Maness was to be best man
at Shirley's marriage to Ruth Desautel, a New Hampshire girl.
Shirley had spent part of the past weekend with Miss Desautel and
had given her their wedding ring. "It'll be safer with you," he told
her.

Like Shirley, nearly every man on board had a station for the
dive. Normally, this wouldn't have been so. Once with the fleet,
the crew would be divided into three watch sections—each on
rotating duty for four hours, each able to dive and surface the
Squalus and operate her whole complex mechanism. But during
these test runs practically everyone was pressed into service. Those
who were not actually at work observed their counterparts in action; still others stood by to take down statistical data for her
official records.

Only two men had no assigned posts today. One was a pharmacist's mate, Raymond O'Hara, who had just joined the crew the
morning before. The other was a cook, Robert Thompson.
Thompson had already been up for hours preparing breakfast.
Finished now at a quarter to eight, he took to his bunk. He told his
relief cook, William Isaacs, that he was going to sleep through the
dive.

The point Naquin had selected for it lay southeast of the
Piscataqua's mouth in an extremely deep stretch of water off the tip
of the Isles of Shoals, a string of rocks running parallel to the
mainland almost six miles away. Naquin wanted room to move
around in; he would have a lot of it. The bottom where he would
dive averaged some 240 feet down, mostly thick blue mud.

Shortly after eight o'clock the Squalus veered to the southeast.
From the bridge atop the conning tower Naquin could see the line
of breakers off to his left pounding against the Shoals. The sun
continued to play a losing game of peekaboo in the overcast sky.

As the *Squalus* bucked ahead on all four diesel engines, the swells cascaded over the teak grating of her deck and streamed down the sides of her rounded black steel hull.

Ten feet above the deck Naquin felt the slap of salt-water spray on his cheeks. In the afternoon he planned a torpedo drill. He hoped the weather wouldn't get any worse. The previous day all eight torpedoes had been recovered after firing and he felt that such efficiency was especially pleasing to Admiral Cole in Portsmouth.

At 8:13 A.M. Naquin ordered a message giving the precise location of the dive radioed back to Portsmouth. But somehow the message as taken down there showed the *Squalus* about five miles east of where she actually submerged.

At 8:30, up on the wind-blown bridge, Lieutenant (j.g.) Robert Robertson took a navigational fix and informed Naquin that they had less than a mile and a half to go on the surface before the *Squalus* reached her point of dive. Naquin ordered his ship readied for submergence. By 8:35 final preparations for her plunge were in full swing. She would be going down in a matter of minutes now.

Naquin's preliminary dive command was received in the control room by his executive officer, Lieutenant Walter Doyle, Jr. Doyle, a tight-lipped black Irishman, was to be in actual charge of the dive this morning. He first ordered the trial crew to man their stations. He next directed all observers to follow suit.

The forward torpedo room had already gone into action. In case Naquin called for a firing three crewmen had just swung a torpedo into reload position under the supervision of a lanky junior-grade lieutenant from Chicago, John Nichols. They were about to start on another when Lieutenant Doyle's order came through so they held off until the *Squalus* completed her dive. Customarily, as Torpedo and Gunnery Officer, Nichols would have been in the

control room at his torpedo data computer, roughly equivalent to
the range finder on a gun. But he wanted to see how the reload
drills were going. He had almost gone back to the after torpedo
room as well; he planned, instead, to look in there during the
afternoon dive. In all his life, Nichols would never make a better
decision.

He checked to make sure the torpedo-tube doors were closed. He
also saw to it that the escape hatch above the forward torpedo room
was locked. Then he stepped back into the forward battery. To his
right, a Filipino mess attendant, Feliciano Elvina, hummed softly
to himself as he soaked out some dirty dishrags in the sink.

Farther back, a hard-bitten chief electrician's mate named Lawrence Gainor, who had served in submarines exactly half of his
forty years, made ready to rattle off meter readings for the forward
battery group. A man stood by to record the figures. Still another
was already waist-down in the hatch to the space below where he
could watch the batteries themselves.

Nichols slipped past them to the control room. He reported to
Doyle that the two forward compartments were rigged for diving.

Ten men waited in the control room to begin the multiple
operations that would take the *Squalus* down. Doyle himself stood
dead center in its forepart. From there, by swiveling his head
slightly, he could see every essential diving control and indicator in
the *Squalus*. At his side was Yeoman Second Class Charles Kuney,
earphones in place, to receive and relay messages throughout the
ship. Harold Preble was also there to observe the dive performance. By perching himself directly behind Doyle, one foot on a
toolbox and the other braced against the bottom rung of the ladder
coming down from the conning tower, he had nearly the same
view. In each hand Preble held a double-action stop watch.

Doyle's order had set the stern compartments in motion as well.
In the after battery, just inside the doorway leading from the

control room, Electrician's Mate Third Class Lloyd Maness got ready to take the same sort of meter readings as Chief Gainor in the forward battery. For Maness, this was old hat. Sherman Shirley's wedding was something else again; Maness had never been a best man before. He thought of all the movies he had seen where the best man couldn't find the ring at the critical moment. It didn't seem so funny now.

Sixteen feet away, on the other side of four stacks of bunks in the middle of the compartment, John Batick drained a cup of coffee, wiped off his mouth with the back of his hand and climbed down the hatch into the after battery space. The hatch was just in front of the mess area where there was considerable traffic, so Batick banged it shut behind him.

At one of the mess tables Seaman First Class William Boulton sat drying off. Boulton had just come from the main deck where he had taken down the flag, stowed away loose lines and bolted the main-deck locker. He could relax now until the *Squalus* surfaced.

In the galley across the way a second Filipino mess attendant aboard, Basilio Galvan, had come back from the forward battery to ask the cook on duty, William Isaacs, what they were going to have for dinner. "Meat balls," Isaacs replied.

Then Galvan hurried forward again. He stepped over the hatch which now enclosed Batick. And as he went past the first tier of bunks on his right he saw the breakfast cook, Robert Thompson, stretched out in one of them. As good as his word, despite all the commotion, Thompson was snoozing peacefully.

Isaacs, with the help of two seamen assigned to him for mess duty, was already hard at work preparing the noon meal. Because of the limited space he had to cook and serve in shifts. He would handle the first batch of hungry crewmen not long after the *Squalus* came up. But with the dive now about to begin he switched off the electric oven. Isaacs had a pan of the meat balls bubbling inside and some of his gravy might spill when the *Squalus* started to go down. He was afraid it would cause a short circuit.

At the rear of the compartment the new man on board, Pharmacist's Mate First Class Raymond O'Hara, had a customer. A twenty-one-year-old seaman named Robert Washburn was complaining about a cold. O'Hara was extra solicitous; the *Squalus* was his first submarine. He took a look at Washburn's tongue. Then he turned to open his medicine cabinet for some pills.

To O'Hara's left a passageway led back to the big diesels that were barreling the *Squalus* along at sixteen knots. Fireman First Class Joshua Casey had donned his battle phone to receive the order to cut them off when she dived. Near him, in the forward engine room, a veteran machinist's mate, Eugene Arthur Hoffman, slowly paced the length of the compartment between his pulsing engines. He felt a proprietary interest in them. The Navy had sent Hoffman to the Cleveland plant of the General Motors Corporation where they were built. For eight months he had watched as they were put together piece by piece, then shipped to Portsmouth and installed in the *Squalus*. In case anything went wrong during the trial runs, a General Motors man, Donald Smith, was on hand to help out. So far, however, they had worked like a charm.

Another man had also been in Cleveland, Chief Machinist's Mate John Chestnutt. For the afternoon dive Chestnutt, who had got his chief's hat only six months before, was ticketed for duty in the control room. But now he stood in the after engine room where Naquin's speed directives from the bridge were translated into fact. Altogether, in the two engine rooms there were eighteen men this morning.

They were under the command of the youngest officer aboard the *Squalus*, Ensign Joseph Patterson. For Patterson, only three years out of Annapolis, it was a plum assignment and the prospects of a brilliant career stretched before him. He had already taken and passed his exams for lieutenant (j.g.) and daily awaited the arrival of his commission papers. He was highly popular with the crew as well, even among some of the old hands who had enlisted around the time he was born. He had close-cropped blond hair and a barrel chest and he moved with the easy grace of an athlete. He had been, as a matter of fact, on the track team at the Naval Academy and was good enough to finish fourth against the world's best in the 400-meter run during the 1936 Berlin Olympics.

When he received Doyle's order to prepare for diving, Patterson began his patrol of the after compartments. In the after torpedo room Torpedoman Second Class Alfred Priester had strapped on his headset and telephone mouthpiece in the event that Naquin wanted to run through a dummy reload drill. Priester boasted tattoos as elegant as those John Batick displayed. On his left forearm he had Popeye; on his right shoulder was a girl entwined by a rose and below it a commemorative wreath encircling the legend "Across the Equator."

Along with the bridegroom-to-be Sherman Shirley, a second man back there, Robert Gibbs, had his mind on a wife. Torpedoman First Class Gibbs had met and married a Rumanian girl while serving with the Asiatic Fleet based at Shanghai. Reassigned to the *Squalus,* he had dropped her off for the time being with his parents in Lexington, South Carolina. But her English was sketchy and it had been an awkward arrangement. Now she was on her way by train to Portsmouth and Gibbs wanted to be at the depot to meet her that night. All morning he had fretted over the thought that Naquin might decide to stay downstream again instead of returning to the Portsmouth Navy Yard.

From the after torpedo room Patterson moved quickly forward through each of the engine rooms and then the after battery. In the control room he personally reported their readiness to Doyle and headed back again to supervise the switch from diesel to battery power.

Less than five minutes had elapsed since Doyle ordered the men to their dive posts. Doyle himself, from his own station, had tested the No. 1 periscope, had seen to it that the ballast-tank and air-pressure men were in position and had checked out the bow and stern planes—the big fins protruding outside the hull that worked in the sea like an airplane's wing flaps. In front of him now, the control board "Christmas tree" confirmed what Nichols and Patterson had reported. The board consisted of red and green lights; each light represented a specific opening in the hull or superstructure of the *Squalus*. Green meant that it was closed and watertight, red showed that it was still open.

On the board only eight lights glowed red at Doyle among all the green. Four marked the exhaust valves for each of the diesel engines. One was for the flapper valve through which the radio antenna rose. Another was for the conning-tower hatch that led to the bridge.

The last two red lights were for a pair of big apertures high up in the conning tower just below the bridge deck. They were called the main or "high" inductions and they would remain open until the *Squalus* began her final glide down. Both were covered by a perforated steel plate and, like any of the other valves on board, they opened and closed essentially the same way those on an ordinary faucet do. From one of them—eighteen inches across—ran the central ventilation system that circulated fresh air through the ship when she rode the surface. The second—a yawning outlet nearly twice as big—funneled air directly back to the diesel engines. This was the same valve whose mechanism had failed to work properly following the first submergence at Portsmouth.

In the control room it grew hushed; just an edge of tension had crept in. "Inform the Captain," Doyle said, "that the ship is rigged for diving." Yeoman Charles Kuney, over his battle phone, relayed the message to Naquin up on the bridge. It was not quite 8:40 A.M.

From the bridge Naquin ordered, "All ahead, emergency." He wanted every bit of momentum the *Squalus* could muster for the dive and she strained forward, past sixteen knots. Next Naquin ordered his final dive message transmitted. In his cubicle at the rear of the control room Radioman Second Class Charles Powell notified Portsmouth that the *Squalus* was now going down. Portsmouth immediately acknowledged. Powell signed off and started to take in his antenna.

Then, still on the bridge, Naquin ordered, "Stand by to dive." He took a last confident look around; the *Squalus* was all by herself except for the two lobstermen now far astern. He slipped through the conning-tower hatch, the last to do so, and with the help of Quartermaster First Class Francis Murphy he pulled it shut. Together they locked it. Just as they did, Naquin heard the big klaxon honk the first diving alarm. He started his stop watch and ducked down the narrow steel ladder toward the control room below.

There Doyle had directed the operators of the bow and stern planes to put them at hard dive. And at his command the main ballast tanks girdling her hull were flooded. They would drag the *Squalus* beneath the surface. Still another big tank, called bow buoyancy, was all the way up forward between the torpedo tubes. It pulled her nose down during a dive. In addition there were several smaller trim and auxiliary tanks for weight adjustment to keep the *Squalus* steady and on an even keel underwater.

The sea entered each of these tanks through a valve set in its lower side. On the upper side of each there was also a vent which allowed air pockets to escape so the tanks could be completely filled. When the *Squalus* was surfacing, the process was reversed. The vents were closed after the dive and blasts of high-pressure air from cylinders manned in the control room blew the sea water out through the same valves by which it had come in.

In quick succession Doyle ordered the valves and vents opened on the bow buoyancy tank and on main ballast tanks 1 and 2. Then he had the valves on tanks 3 and 4 also opened; this would partially flood them. He held back opening their vents until he was absolutely certain that the *Squalus* was watertight.

The control board would tell him that. And his eyes never left it. He now saw the light for the conning-tower hatch wink from red to green after Naquin and Murphy closed it. So did the one for the radio antenna. Then those for the diesel engine exhausts went green. In the control room there was a startling silence when the diesels cut off; it made everybody's breathing sound very loud.

On the control board only two lights still glowed red—those for the two main inductions set beneath the bridge deck. Both closed simultaneously from the same hydraulic lever in the control room. Machinist's Mate Second Class Alfred Prien would operate it this morning. He had had the same duty in another submarine before reporting to the *Squalus*. Prien now pulled the lever and the last two red lights on the board turned green.

Doyle shut his eyes for one count and then looked at his board again; it was all green. The *Squalus* was secure. To make doubly sure, Carol Pierce, Machinist's Mate Second Class, bled some air from one of the high-pressure cylinders used to blast water out of the ballast tanks. If pressure built up inside the hull, it meant it was airtight and therefore watertight. From his perch behind Doyle, Pierce announced, "Pressure in the boat, sir."

Eyes still on the board, Doyle raised his right hand and extended two fingers. At the signal Chief Torpedoman Roy Campbell, the ranking enlisted man on board, pressed a button that set the big klaxon off the second time. Doyle then ordered the vents on main ballast tanks 3 and 4 opened.

Now on battery power, the *Squalus* slid down into the ocean. Outside, the Atlantic boiled over her elongated hull, reached for her three-inch deck gun and surged up around the base of her conning tower. Then, suddenly, she was gone.

In the control room, after sounding the second alarm, Chief Campbell instinctively glanced at the board and saw it was green. Yeoman Kuney saw it was green. Kuney always liked to bet with himself whether he would ever get word of a valve closing over the battle phone before it registered on the board. The board always won. Alfred Prien, who had pulled the lever to close the main inductions, saw that the board was green. So did Harold Preble. You could almost taste it as the tension eased.

Just as the klaxon went off the second time, Lieutenant Naquin reached the bottom rung of the ladder in the control room on his way down from the conning tower. He, too, saw that there were no red lights on the board. Naquin stepped past Preble and joined Doyle at the diving-control station. He kept his eyes on the depth-gauge indicator in front of him.

When it registered twenty-eight feet, the *Squalus* hesitated. This habitually happened during a dive. It signified the end of her initial thrust from the surface. Now, against the mounting pressure of the sea from below, it took a few seconds for her battery power to assert itself. Then she plunged on down again. At thirty feet, Preble said to Naquin, "You're going to make it."

"This," Naquin replied, "is going to be a beauty."

The depth indicator moved faster . . . thirty-five feet . . . forty . . . forty-five. Up inside the conning tower, Lieutenant (j.g.) Robert Robertson saw the sea flash over his eyeports. Doyle, meanwhile, had his bow and stern plane operators gradually reduce the dive angle. He wanted the *Squalus* to level off completely at around sixty-three feet.

At fifty feet, their time-target depth, both Naquin and Preble called out, "Mark!" They stopped their watches simultaneously and compared the results. The dive had taken precisely one minute and two seconds. "Extra good," said Preble. Naquin smiled. Automatically, he stepped back to his No. 1 periscope, gripped its handles and bent slightly forward to take a look through the rubber-cupped eyepiece.

As he did, a strange fluttering assailed his ears.

An instant later Yeoman Charles Kuney's eyes went wide with disbelief, not at what he saw but what he heard. For the first time something had come over his battle phone that *didn't* show up on the control board. Kuney blurted out the words numbly, "Sir! The engine rooms—they're flooding!"

Everybody in the control room froze, hypnotized by the control board. It was still unaccountably green. There was a moment of complete stupefaction on all their faces, the kind experienced by men who are absolutely sure that what is coming to pass cannot possibly be; yet it was.

Somehow, the dreadful thing had happened. The big thirty-one-inch main air-induction valve leading back to the now-dormant diesels had failed to close or, if it did close, had opened again. With terrible force, tons of sea water shot into the engine rooms. It was as if a huge fire hydrant, wide open, had suddenly gone berserk. The fluttering sensation Naquin had felt an instant before was the rush of air being shoved violently forward by the ocean as it burst in on the after sections of the *Squalus*.

Naquin was the first to recover. "Blow all main ballast!" he shouted. The words were barely out of his mouth before Doyle echoed them, adding, "Blow bow buoyancy!" The still-mesmerized control-room crew came to and scrambled into action. Alfred Prien had already closed off the air-escape vents in the ballast tanks. Now Carol Pierce, his hand resting by chance on the lever that would blow 3,000 pounds per square inch of air into the bow buoyancy tank, slammed it home. The air from his No. 1 cylinder, or bank, blasted off. Inside the control room it made a soft hissing sound. A moment later, he sent more air under pressure rushing into the main ballast tanks to drive the sea from them.

Without being told, Gunner's Mate First Class Eugene Cravens and Machinist's Mate Second Class Gavin Coyne, operating the bow and stern dive planes, immediately put them at hard rise. After that all they could do was to hang on helplessly. Prien, having closed the ballast-tank air vents, now could not stop looking down dumbly at the lever that should have shut both main inductions. He clenched it, knuckles white, and tried to yank it farther toward him. But it wouldn't budge; it was down as far as it could go. Yeoman Kuney stood transfixed, his hands clapped over his telephone receivers, pressing them tighter to his ears. The last thing he heard from the after compartments was an awful scream, "Take her up! Take her up!" Kuney couldn't tell which compartment the scream had come from.

The *Squalus* shuddered.

At eighty feet, for a desperate tick in time, she hung suspended between ocean floor and surface. Then she responded to the blowing of her ballast tanks. Her bow tilted sharply upward. She even climbed a little, her nose perhaps just breaking through the waves above. But the growing weight in her tail was too much. Inexorably now, she began to slide stern down into the black depths of the North Atlantic.

The steep pitch of the *Squalus* came so suddenly that only by clinging to his No. 1 periscope and bracing himself against the steel well of the second periscope directly behind did Naquin remain on his feet. How—the question pounded in his brain— could this have happened?

As Carol Pierce sent emergency blasts of air into the ballast tanks, Harold Preble rushed to his aid. Hanging on to the base of the gyrocompass with one hand, he knelt beside Pierce and tried to cut in a reserve supply of air to clear the tanks faster. He had to use a wrench to get the valve open. He was still struggling with it when a column of water hit him in the back of the neck and flattened him. Both Pierce and Chief Roy Campbell were doused by the same stream. Pierce, stumbling over Preble, grabbed the wrench and finished the job; it was a futile effort.

Campbell picked Preble up. Then he reached overhead to block off a pipeline in the ventilation system where the water had come through. By now the sea had found its way into the maze of pipes that ran the length of the *Squalus*. In the control room jets of water sprayed from half a dozen different places. The men worked frantically to shut them off, grabbing hold of whatever they could to stay upright.

Behind him, Chief Campbell heard an ominous hissing. He traced it back to the two water closets in the rear of the control room on the starboard side. Inside, Campbell groped through a billowing mist. It was coming out of a drainage line in the second closet. He had trouble turning the handwheel that shut the valve; the new packing around it made it stick. But he finally did it. Then he turned off every other valve he could find.

Across from Campbell, in his radio cubicle, Radioman Charles Powell was still putting away his transmitter after sending the dive message when water gushed out of an air-supply blower in front of him. Powel reached up toward a valve in the pipe that he thought might stop the flow. Before he got to it, however, the water suddenly dwindled to a dribble. Powell figured somebody in the after battery had closed another valve farther down the line. He sealed his anyway and then staggered into the control room proper. There the overhead lights flickered, flared for an instant and went out. The emergency lights came on. They, too, began to flicker.

Up front in the forward torpedo room, when the bow rose abruptly, Torpedoman Third Class Leonard de Medeiros wondered why they were surfacing so soon. The harrowing answer came over the battle phone. Lieutenant Nichols immediately ordered de Medeiros to close the watertight door between the forward torpedo room and the forward battery.

A second later the dummy torpedo set up for the reload started to roll free. Loose in there with the *Squalus* tilting crazily, it would crush anyone in its path. Nichols, Torpedoman Second Class William Fitzpatrick and Seaman First Class Donato Persico all jumped for it and wrestled it back in place. Nichols finally threaded its nose ring with manila line and together the three men managed to lash the torpedo down. By then some sea water mixed with air began to spurt out of the ventilation pipes, but it didn't amount to much. De Medeiros quickly shut the valves and the spray of water stopped completely. Now, bracing themselves against the downward slide of the *Squalus,* all the men in the forward torpedo room could do in the eerie silence was wait. And hope.

In the forward battery, as the *Squalus* fought to rise, a coffee pot whistled past Mess Attendant First Class Feliciano Elvina from one side of the pantry to the other. Elvina picked up the pot and tried to set in on its stand; it toppled over again. He put it down in a corner on the deck. To his intense annoyance water suddenly belched out of the faucet into the sink all over the dishrags he had squeezed dry a minute before.

Muttering under his breath, Elvina stuck his head into the passageway to see what was up. Farther back everyone seemed to be yelling, but Elvina was no great shakes at English and he could not understand what they were saying. Then he saw the face of the second mess attendant, his friend Basilio Galvan, pop out of the ship's office. Elvina looked questioningly at him. Galvan had been in submarines before and this was Elvina's first. Galvan simply shrugged, however, and Elvina couldn't tell whether or not he was concerned. Galvan was concerned *and* confused by the sudden turn of events, but as a veteran submariner in Elvina's eyes he was determined not to show his ignorance. Finally Elvina just gave up, went back into the pantry and hunched down next to his coffeepot.

Machinist's Mate Second Class Allen Bryson was on the forward battery phone when he heard the same terrible scream from the engine rooms that Yeoman Kuney heard. Bryson shouted the news. Gerald McLees, Electrician's Mate Second Class, still hadn't got all the way through the hatch leading to the battery space when he heard it. Forthwith, McLees scrambled back up into the passageway. Standing by his voltmeters, Chief Lawrence Gainor had yet to relay one reading to his recorder, a signalman named Theodore Jacobs. But Gainor would have his hands full soon enough.

Sometimes a man's heroic moment comes upon him so suddenly that he has no chance to think about it. All his training comes into instinctive play, activated by whatever the chemistry is that makes one man charge and another run, one man grapple with opportunity and another impotent. For Lawrence Gainor that moment had arrived. At the first word of trouble he had secured the watertight door between the forward battery and the control room with the help of Jacobs. Then, as the overhead lights flickered, he took another look at his voltmeters. They were discharging at a furious rate. Somewhere along the line there was a bad short circuit. Gainor grabbed a flashlight and pulled himself forward against the upward slant of the *Squalus* to the battery hatch. When he peered down, he was greeted by a fearful sight. The batteries had shorted. Solid bands of blue-white fire were leaping from battery to battery in eight-inch arcs. Jumping through the blackness, they threw grotesque shadows on the sides of the space. The heat was so intense that steam now poured out of the battery cells and the rubber-compound insulation had begun to melt. As the *Squalus* continued her sickening drop, she was only seconds away from a gigantic explosion that would rip her apart even before she reached the bottom.

Gainor climbed down the ladder. The big batteries completely filled the space beneath the deck. Alone, squinting against the fiery bands of electricity leaping around him, he crouched over them on a narrow walk and groped grimly for the master disconnect switches. Finally he found the starboard switch and yanked it clear. Next he bent to his left for the port switch. A terrifying arc over it sputtered and flashed in his face; one brush against it would send him to a horrible death. Gainor was sure he would be burned before he could reach the switch. He tried anyway and with a last desperate effort he jerked it free. The fierce arcs dropped away as swiftly as they had come. In the forward compartments all the lights went out. Then Gainor quietly made his way back up the ladder.

In the after battery, on the other side of the control room, Electrician's Mate Third Class Lloyd Maness faced as hair-raising a job. Like Gainor, Maness was set to call off voltmeter readings during the dive. He never got to the first one. For both Maness and his recorder, Radioman First Class Arthur Booth, the early stages of the dive were perfectly familiar. Booth, his pencil out, had noted down the time in Navyese—0841. Together they now waited for the meter indicator to settle down. Through the open doorway they could hear Lieutenant Doyle issuing orders to the control-room crew.

Suddenly the same movement of air that assailed Naquin's ears went sweeping by them. Then they heard Kuney's stunned cry that the engine rooms were flooding. An instant later all hell broke loose in the after battery. The lights went out almost immediately.

Maness reached for the emergency-light switch and turned it on. In the dim glow, water seemed to be shooting in everywhere. Maness moved swiftly to his disaster station, the watertight door between the after battery and the control room. He stepped into the control room and got ready to swing it shut.

As he did, Booth jumped past him.

Farther back in the after battery, Electrician's Mate First Class Judson Bland was manning the compartment battle phone. When he heard the incredible report come over it, he couldn't believe his ears. Then the water hit him. Bland's first thought was to close the valves in the overhead ventilation pipes. But he had not been on dive duty in the after battery before and he wasn't quite sure where they were. As he felt for them in the half light of the emergency lamps, the *Squalus* lurched violently up and sent him skidding to his knees. By now he realized that she was long past the point where closing off some valves would do any good, and as the full impact of what had happened swept over him, Bland scrambled toward the control room. Maness yelled at him to hurry.

Seaman William Boulton came on desperately behind Bland. One minute Boulton had been sitting at a mess table, staring idly into space. In the next, he was dumfounded to see water streaming down the after battery deck. For a moment he could think only that the main-deck hatch above him had not been secured. He stood up automatically to check it. As he did, the sea rocketed in from pipes all over the compartment. And almost before he knew it the water level had surged over the tops of his work shoes. Boulton started splashing his way forward against the upward incline of the *Squalus*. The water was pouring in faster now, springing suddenly at him from a dozen directions. Dazed by its terrifying crossfire, Boulton kept going blindly. Then, all at once, he had passed Maness and stumbled into the control room.

At the far end of the after battery, Seaman Second Class Robert

Washburn was still waiting for the pharmacist's mate, O'Hara, to give him his cold pills when the water came in. It shot out of the air blower over the medicine cabinet with explosive force, slamming Washburn to the deck on the portside of the compartment. He struggled to his feet just as the *Squalus* rose by her bow and was thrown headlong to the deck again. Once more he managed to struggle up.

O'Hara was searching through his cabinet as the water gushed over his head, barely missing him. Then the bottles on the shelves started tumbling out. Instinctively O'Hara tried to catch them. A moment later he found himself sitting on the deck, the water swirling around his wrist. He flopped around and pushed himself up with both hands. He saw Washburn a little to his right ahead of him and he started to follow his erstwhile patient. By this time the slant of the *Squalus* was so steep that Washburn had to cling to the bunks lining the compartment as he worked himself forward hand over hand, O'Hara a few feet behind, and finally he fell into the control room. Lloyd Maness, holding the door, urged O'Hara on. At last O'Hara, too, staggered past him.

In the galley William Isaacs, the cook, waited impatiently for the *Squalus* to level off so he could switch his oven on again. Isaacs had a seaman, Alexander Keegan, along with Fireman Second Class Roland Blanchard, helping on mess duty. When the *Squalus* began her dive, Keegan had left to go to the crew's toilet across the passageway. Isaacs and Blanchard never saw him again.

After the first sound of the klaxon, Blanchard had stopped his potato peeling and started closing a valve in the hull ventilation line running through the galley. This was one of his regular dive assignments and, as had happened on previous plunges, he ran into trouble trying to turn the stiff, new handwheel. There was a quick rush of escaping air and then the water followed. Blanchard put everything he had into it but there was so much pressure now that he couldn't budge the wheel at all.

At the first unexpected whoosh of air Isaacs looked inquiringly into the passageway outside the galley. A solid stream of water smacked him in the face. He ducked away and glanced aft toward the forward engine room. The door to it was shut but not bolted; more water was spurting through from the other side. Isaacs moved quickly to it and secured the door. Then he straightened up to look through the eyeport. The sight was awesome. A great cataract was thundering out of the air-induction outlet above the diesels. It had already buried them. Isaacs stood there bewitched.

In the galley Blanchard had given up trying to turn the hand-wheel and came into the passageway. When the *Squalus* tipped up, all the water in the after battery came racing down the deck toward him. Blanchard waded forward, fighting the current, arms flailing wildly to keep his balance. He had gotten about a third of the way through the compartment when he slipped. His head went under and he felt himself being carried back again. At the last second his hand clutched a steel stanchion. He hung on and then with savage frenzy he pulled himself up. Kicking off from the stanchion, he lunged desperately for the nearest tier of bunks. He made it and dragged himself from one tier to the next. The water wasn't as deep here but it kept pouring down from the pipes overhead and the footing was miserable. Up ahead he saw the door to the control room begin to close. He yelled out. And Maness heard him. The door hesitated and then eased open.

For Isaacs, meanwhile, time was fast running out. But, his face pressed against the eyeport, he seemed unable to tear himself away from the frightful sight inside the forward engine room. He could not see anyone, just the thundering ocean. Then at last he became aware of the icy water lapping around his waist. Before he could move, it had almost reached his armpits. He frantically propelled himself away from the door, actually swimming, and barged right into one of the mess tables hidden by the rising tide. Isaacs went under, but he had a hand around a leg of the table bolted to the deck and he came up spewing salt water from his mouth. He kept going and Maness, holding the door open an instant longer, saw him. Isaacs floundered into the rear of the control room and fell to his knees, gasping for breath.

Now Maness could delay no more.

Twice he had paused before sealing off the control room, once for Blanchard, then for Isaacs. He peered into the darkness of the after battery. Nobody else was coming. Even if there was somebody, he would not be able to wait. His task was tremendous. The door swung in from the after battery. It was oval and fitted into a steel frame that curved around the rest of the passageway. Normally, when the *Squalus* was on an even keel, it moved easily on its hinges, but now the ravaged ship sagged by her stern at nearly a fifty-degree angle. Maness had to lift it toward him almost as if it were a trap door. A trap door of solid steel except for its eyeport, weighing several hundred pounds.

And he had to do it alone; there wasn't enough room in the passageway for anyone to help him. Maness bent forward and pulled, the sea already spilling over the lip of the doorway. He strained harder. Beads of sweat popped full-blown across his face. The door began to swing up steadily, inch by inch. Then it stopped, neither moving up nor falling back, three-quarters of the way closed. Maness gritted his teeth. Summoning a last ferocious burst of strength, his arm and shoulder muscles quivering wildly, he heaved once more. This time the door shut. Somewhere on the other side, he knew, was Sherman Shirley. Before the dive Shirley had mentioned something about the wedding ceremony. Now Maness couldn't remember what it was.

Moments later, in a swirl of trailing bubbles, the *Squalus* touched delicately on the bottom, first her stern, then her bow. Inside they hardly felt it. She settled evenly on her keel, still slanting up at an angle of about eleven degrees. Her emergency lights were out and she had no heat. She lay helpless in 243 feet of water. The temperature outside her hull was a degree above freezing.

In the control room Chief Roy Campbell held a flashlight up to the eyeport of the door Maness had closed; an evil film of oily water rode against it on the other side. It was not quite 8:45 A.M. Less than five minutes had slipped by since the *Squalus* started her dive. Up on the surface it was as if she had never existed at all.

2

AT THE WASHINGTON NAVY YARD SHORTLY BEFORE ONE o'clock in the afternoon, Swede Momsen was working his way through the second of the two ham sandwiches on hard rolls that he favored for lunch. A diver in the pressure tank on helium and oxygen was simulating an ascent from 250 feet and had another hour to go before he would be out. Aside from a ripple of kidding when he showed up that morning in his panama hat, Momsen's day this May 23rd had been uneventful. And as soon as the man in the tank was finished, he planned to call it quits and get home early as he had promised his wife.

Then the phone rang. Momsen happened to pick up the receiver himself, idly thinking it must be a girl friend of one of his young divers. They had a habit of calling around lunchtime. On the other end, instead, was the tense voice of the Navy Department's Commander Charles Lockwood. Lockwood wasted no words. "Swede," he said, "there's hell to pay. The *Squalus* is down off Portsmouth."

"How deep?" Momsen asked instantly.

"We don't know," Lockwood said. "But deep, I'm afraid. Somewhere between two hundred and four hundred feet. She went down near the Isles of Shoals. We're getting a plane ready now. There's room for you and three others. We'll get the rest of your people up as soon as we can. If I have anything more, I'll get right back to you."

With infinite care Momsen put the phone down.

So it had finally happened. After fourteen years the day had come. And despite the jeers and the backbiting and the skeptics, all the work was suddenly not in vain—the long days and restless nights of dreaming and planning, the time after time he had risked his own neck to save those of others. A brassbound superior once said with a sneer, "Who does this guy Momsen think he is, Jules Verne?"

But without him now there would have been no hope for the crew of the *Squalus*. Momsen, that fateful Tuesday, knew more about underwater escape and rescue than anyone else on earth. Everything that could possibly help get those men out—smoke bombs, telephone marker buoys, new diving techniques, escape hatches and artificial lungs, the great pear-shaped rescue chamber —was either a direct result of his pioneer work or of value only because of it. None had ever been used before in an actual submarine disaster. Now they would be. And under the worst imaginable conditions—in fickle weather, the water bitterly cold, the men awesomely far down.

Until Momsen came along, scant attention was paid to the question of saving submariners. You simply took your chances. If your boat went down—as they did with nerve-racking regularity— you were fortunate to die quickly, by drowning. If you didn't, you usually suffocated. Once in a while sheer luck—and makeshift ingenuity—got you out alive.

There was the *O-5*, rammed by a United Fruit freighter. But she foundered in the clear, calm waters of a bay at the Atlantic end of the Panama Canal. She was only thirty feet down on a sand bottom within easy reach of two of the canal's giant floating cranes, the *Ajax* and the *Hercules*. Cables were slipped around her bow, the cranes hoisted her clear of the water and those trapped inside climbed out. There was the *S-5*. She dived innocently into the Atlantic off Cape May, New Jersey, with her torpedo room still open to the sea. Her crew made it safely aft, however, and she lay in water shallow enough for her tail to break the surface when she blew her stern ballast tanks. From within they drilled a hole in her hull and stuck out a length of pipe with a white shirt fluttering from it. Finally a Swedish merchantman lumbered by to take a closer look at the strange sight; then the sea remained miraculously placid while rescuers cut a larger opening in her exposed stern so the men could wriggle out one by one. There was also Momsen's own *O-15*, his first command. Trying for a time record, he plunged her steeply into the Atlantic off Coco Solo, Panama, at full power. When he ordered her leveled off, the bow planes suddenly jammed and she kept going down. Her motors were frantically reversed but it was too late. She slammed into the bottom, her bow buried some thirty feet in mud and held fast by it. In the desperate time that followed, Momsen grimly sought a way out; at last he hit upon an ingenious solution. Despite the mud, he was able to ease each of the *O-15*'s outside torpedo-tube doors partially open. Then he carefully flooded the tubes. When he blasted the water out of the first tube, as if he were firing a torpedo, nothing happened. Nor did it after the second. After firing the third tube the *O-15* quivered slightly. With the fourth blast there was another, stronger movement. Everyone on board held a collective breath. Then the bow slowly floated free.

These were some of the happy endings. But there was also the *S-*

51 moving along the Atlantic surface one night in 1925 off Block
Island when she was ripped apart by the passenger ship *City of
Rome*. As skipper of a sister ship, the *S-1*, it was Momsen himself
who was destined to find her telltale oil slick and the ugly air
bubbles rising from the bottom 131 feet down. Recalling the scene
later in a letter to a friend, he wrote: "We tried to contact her but
there was only silence. Those of us on the bridge of the *S-1* simply
stared at the water and said nothing at first. No one at that time
knew anything about the principles of escape and rescue. We were
utterly helpless."

He remembered something else, too. Months afterward he
would learn of the horribly contorted faces and the flesh-shredded
hands of those who had not drowned immediately, who instead
had spent the last minutes of their lives trying to claw a way out
of their steel coffin.

Two years later the *S-4*'s number was up. On a trial run one
December afternoon off Provincetown, Massachusetts, just a
couple of feet below the surface, she was slashed open by the Coast
Guard destroyer *Paulding* out chasing prohibition rumrunners.
Incredibly, all forty men on board were still alive as she lay on the
bottom, only 110 feet down—less than the distance from home
plate to second base—a score of ships hovering above her. But they
could do nothing, and a howling winter gale wiped out what little
chance there was of raising her. For nearly three days the en-
tombed men beat out their pitiful hammer taps of hope inside her
hull. Each hour the taps grew more feeble. Then they stopped
altogether.

And now it was the *Squalus*.

Momsen's career in the Navy, ironically, was almost ended
before it began. He entered Annapolis in 1914. In the spring, at
the end of his plebe year, a cheating scandal erupted at the Naval

Academy and midyear exams the following winter were made doubly difficult. All told, nearly three hundred midshipmen failed and were forced to resign. Momsen, who had just missed a passing grade in Spanish, was one of them. He immediately tried for a reappointment from his home district congressman in St. Paul, Minnesota. His case seemed hopeless. The Republican who originally appointed him had been subsequently defeated—by a Democrat. To make matters worse, Momsen's father was active in local G.O.P. politics. Momsen nonetheless displayed the same dogged determination that would mark his entire naval career. He pursued the new representative from St. Paul to Washington and back again, pleading his cause. The congressman, Carl C. Van Dyke, finally acquiesced, noting in a letter to Momsen's father, "I want to make it perfectly clear that . . . the only reason for my reappointing your son, Charles, is because of Charles himself."

As a member of the class of 1920, Momsen had to repeat his plebe year. But because of World War I he actually graduated and was commissioned an ensign in 1919. Kept on at Annapolis to help organize the incoming crop of plebes, he started tinkering with the Navy at once by instituting the practice—still in effect—of allowing midshipmen to walk off demerits instead of having them charged against class standing. He next spent two humdrum years aboard a brace of battlewagons, the *Oklahoma* and the *Maryland*. Then one spring day in 1921 he spotted a fleet circular that shaped his whole future. A new class of recruits was being accepted for training at the submarine school in New London, Connecticut. Momsen applied forthwith. In those days submarine service had something less than élite status. The captain of the spanking-new *Maryland* made this quite clear. "Better reconsider, young man," he counseled. "Only the scum of the Navy go into submarines."

The *Maryland*'s skipper could hardly be blamed. You had to be a little offbeat to become a submariner. All the Navy's pride was centered around its big battle line; submarines were grudgingly tolerated as a new sea weapon but sort of underhanded when you came right down to it, and hardly the place for a rising young officer and gentleman. An Annapolis man faced double jeopardy when he joined up. He not only had to undergo the tremendous risks involved but he wound up scraping the bottom of the Navy's social barrel as well.

Living conditions, moreover, were wretched. When Swede Momsen boarded his first submarine, she was a cramped capsule half the size of the *Squalus*. His berth was a collapsible cot alongside a torpedo. His belongings remained in the suitcase he brought with him. There was only a washbasin and no shower. Laundry facilities were nonexistent. Because of the arduous duty there were extra food rations, but this didn't mean much in practice. There was no refrigeration and fresh meat usually spoiled before it could be cooked. When it did, the job of hauling it up the hatches to be tossed overboard was a memorable one. Butter, stored in half-gallon cans, sloshed around completely liquefied after a day or so. Fresh water, since there were no distillers, was limited to the amount you could carry with you; it wasn't bad when it was cooked with coffee. Air conditioning was a subject reserved for your wildest daydreams and the aroma inside the hull, a combination of fuel fumes, sweat and dirty socks, was something you never really got used to. To top things off there were no toilets. When traveling submerged, you were reduced to a bucket half filled with diesel oil. "Even goldfish stink in diesel oil," an old-time chief observed. On the surface you draped yourself over the main-deck railing and were interrupted more often than not by a breaking swell. The upshot was a defiant ditty:

> Submarines have no latrines.
> The men wear leathern britches.
> They hang their tails out o'er the rails
> And yell like sons-o-bitches.

Despite such drawbacks, submarine service was difficult to get into. The physical requirements were formidable and the psychological stress of close confinement often proved unbearable. But for those who made it, a raffish *élan* emerged out of all the discomfort that was unequaled elsewhere in the Navy. For some there was a sense of riding the wave of the future. For others the lure of danger was excitement enough. More tangible benefits resulted as well. Submarine sailors suffered practically none of the stuffy discipline that was *de rigueur* on most surface ships. They got fairly rapid promotions and also additional pay; each day's diving was worth an extra dollar, "not to exceed fifteen dollars a month." Officers, for their part, could live at home between sea trips. Most important, they had a chance to command while still relatively junior in rank.

How to get out of a submarine—in case something went haywire—was a question nobody wanted to dwell on. When Momsen was in submarine school, the problem was pointedly ducked. Sometimes in the dead of night you couldn't help thinking about the tons of water that enveloped you only a few inches away. From there it was no trick to picture yourself hopelessly trapped on the ocean floor. But it was considered bad form to talk about it. Whenever a new catastrophe struck, you simply took the tack that it wouldn't happen to you. Or you got philosophical. After all, ran the argument, you could be knocked off just as easily crossing a street.

Swede Momsen was no different from the rest. And the chances are he might never have changed had not a curious web of coincidence centered on a man of precisely his talent and temperament. Indeed, looking back, it would appear that it had all been carefully ordained without his having any real choice in the matter.

Within eighteen months, as a new junior lieutenant, he was handed his first command, the aged *O-15*. It was a heady time.

Even given the chafing limitations of his creaky craft, he was held
spellbound by the enormous potential that lay beneath the surface.
If he thought at all about the perils that rode with him on every
trip he showed no sign of it. Not even his own chilling plunge
into the mud dismayed him; he just chalked it up as one of those
things. For the husky young skipper with cheerful blue eyes, being
aboard a submarine was the best of all possible lives.

Nothing, it seemed, could dim his delight. Bound north for
Philadelphia, the *O-15* chugged out of the Gulf of Mexico late one
October afternoon. The air grew heavy and a long, oily swell
rolled out of the southeast. During the night the wind rose in the
north, picked up even more and then backed eastward. Before
daybreak it was at gale force and the sea built steadily higher. The
O-15 was caught in the maw of a monstrous hurricane. By noon
she was lurching in dizzy sweeps up and down the huge combers
and Momsen had what he thought must be the sickest crew in all
history on his hands. It was pointless to submerge. The old *O-15*
could not go deep enough to escape such gigantic wave action.
Besides, this looked like a really big blow, and if she surfaced with
her battery gone and the storm still raging, she would be helpless.
Momsen could only try to ride it out. First he wedged a wooden
plank across the conning-tower hatch to allow air down inside the
hull while keeping most of the solid water out. Then he lashed
himself to the bridge with double lengths of manila line. The sea
ran higher and higher and the wind shrieked poisonously past him.
Whole mountains of water heaved skyward, hesitated and then
came hurtling down on him. Momsen had never seen anything like
them. They seemed a hundred feet high. Each time the *O-15* was
buried in their swirling mass, he held his breath; each time he was
sure he would never come up. The hurricane raged unbelievably on
through the day and by dark it was stronger than ever. In the
fading light, he now saw his main-deck railing bent all the way

over, and around the bridge the protective sheet metal was crumpled and battered like paper.

It kept up through the night as well, the *O-15* first bucking, then rolling forty and fifty degrees at a clip. Around 5 A.M. she entered the eye of the storm. The wind stopped suddenly. The sea was nearly flat. The sky above Momsen had a pale greenish glow; he found it eerily oppressive. From the bridge he called down a warning to get ready for more. In less than half an hour the respite was over and the wind roared in from the opposite direction. Seconds later the colossal waves hit with even greater fury. All that day the *O-15* continued to reel under the fearful pounding. Finally, after dark, the winds slowed and the sea began to ease a little. Momsen had been lashed to the bridge for nearly thirty-five sleepless hours, sustained only by an occasional onion sandwich, his favorite food in foul weather, thrust up through the hatch by a mess steward. Now, with the end in sight, he sent for the only other officer he had, an ensign fresh from submarine school, to take over. The ensign wobbled up and weakly saluted, barely able to talk, much less stand. When the *O-15* at last limped into port, the new man promptly put in for a transfer. He didn't care where, he said, just as far away as possible from submarines.

But for Momsen this whole hurricane simply set the stage for a dénouement he loved to tell. After going below he had found an unholy mess. Men all around him groaned and retched miserably. With every pitch and roll of the ship an assortment of gear, overturned vomit buckets and forlorn bits of clothing sloshed freely back and forth. It was even worse in the galley, the deck a slimy conglomeration of prunes, beans, bread, broken crockery and drifting pots. Yet still on duty by the range, splattered with grease and bloody from a cut on his forehead, was the cook. With one hand he gripped a pipe for support while in the other he triumphantly juggled a panful of frying potatoes. "There will always be a special berth in heaven," Momsen noted with a flourish in his diary, "for a submarine cook."

Such carefree exuberance would soon be badly jolted. And afterward Swede Momsen would never again be quite the same man. In the summer of 1925 he had come up to the big submarine base at New London to take command of the *S-1*. Now a full lieutenant, he was elated by the assignment. Although the *S* boats, a World War I design, had multiple shortcomings, they were still the best the submarine service, at the mercy of Navy appropriations, could boast. Besides, the *S-1* had an added attraction; a large tank holding a collapsible pontoon scout plane was bolted to her deck and he looked forward to working on the experimental project.

Then on September 25th the base duty officer roused him at home a little after 3 A.M. with forbidding news. The *S-51*, out on a night practice run, had been rammed and probably sunk by the *City of Rome* east of Block Island. Momsen blinked wide awake in consternation. The *S-51* was in his division and packed with close personal friends. He mumbled that he'd be right down.

Once the *S-1* was under way, manned by her watch crew, Momsen's eyes strained against the darkness. But there was nothing in sight as he raced toward the supposed point of collision and no sound save the throb of his own diesels. Then, at sunrise, he reached the spot. Bobbing in the waves was a marker buoy dropped by the *City of Rome*. That was all. Momsen slowly picked his way through the area around the buoy. Still nothing. He called off his fruitless sweeps and began instead to trail along the *City of Rome*'s last reported course, thinking that perhaps she might have carried the stricken *S-51* with her for a while.

He guessed right. Two miles northeast of the buoy one of his lookouts spied an oil slick. And the eddying air bubbles. Momsen circled the glistening stain, probing for pieces of wreckage. Or bodies. There were none. He radioed word of his appalling find back to New London and was ordered to stay put until relief arrived. He moved in closer to the oil slick and cautiously lowered his anchor. Then he tried reaching the *S-51* with his underwater oscillator; it sent sound signals fanning through the sea. Over and over again he pinged out her call letters. There was no response. A savage sense of futility swept over him. But there was nothing he could do now except wait. And when the rest of the ships came, that was about all they could do, too. One of his crewmen, staring down at the air bubbles, finally cried, "Oh my God, oh my God." Momsen told him to go below. As much to himself as to the others on the bridge, he said, "At least it was fast. They probably never realized what happened."

Still, he had known them so well. Especially a young lieutenant like himself named Haselden: James Dudley Haselden. They were classmates at Annapolis. They attended submarine school at the same time. They even took their first training cruise together. And before the *S-51* salvage was over, he would also know just how Haselden died, his fingers pathetically torn; in his final moments before blacking out he had tried to pry open an escape hatch, a hatch held shut by more than fifteen tons of ocean pressure. Momsen thought he was going to throw up.

In the fitful nights that followed, the faces of his friends swam through his dreams. By day a mounting anger dogged him. Somehow there had to be a way to save men like Haselden and the others. Or at least give them a fighting chance for survival. But what? For weeks he wrestled with the problem, ruthlessly discarding idea after idea. At last the glimmer of a workable plan began to form in his mind. The more he thought about it, the better it looked.

The concept was simple. It consisted of a large steel rescue chamber, shaped like a bell, capable of being lowered from the surface along guidelines that were attached to ringbolts on the deck of the submarine. Once the bell was in place and the hatch opened, rescuers would be able to get into the hull compartments or the trapped men could climb out on their own.

To do it Momsen planned on having a flat steel plate, something like a washer, welded around all submarine hatches. When the bell landed on the plate, the hatch proper would be enclosed by it. He also designed a rubber gasket around the bottom of the bell to help guarantee a watertight hookup. After the bell was directly over the hatch, the air pressure inside—until then equal to that of the surrounding water—would be reduced. This would seal the bell to the hatch plate. If the submarine was partially flooded, however, its combined water and air pressure might be enough to break the seal after the hatch was opened. So he took a final precaution. The bell would be bolted down before anybody touched the hatch.

Momsen ran over the whole thing time and again. Then he hashed it over with a dozen or so of his fellow skippers. None of them could see anything wrong with it. Thus heartened, he set the scheme down on paper in considerable detail and worked up a number of accompanying sketches. Next he took the complete package to the base commander at New London, Captain Ernest J. King. King, who would become the Navy's World War II chief, was immediately intrigued. "Swede," he said, "I think you've got a hell of an idea." He promptly forwarded the plan to the Navy Bureau of Construction and Repair for appraisal, along with an endorsement couched in more official language: "The subject device is the most practicable one for the rescue of entrapped submarine crews available. . . ."

Nothing happened. At first this didn't bother Momsen; he had no reason to expect an early response. Analysis, after all, took time. But as the weeks turned to months and the months stretched into almost a year, his disappointment deepened. There must have been a radical defect nobody in New London noticed and he was right back where he started. He promised himself that he would begin working up another escape project he had bouncing around in the back of his head. It was hard, however, to get going on it, not knowing what the trouble had been with the bell.

Then he found out. And in a way he would never suspect. He was due for a tour of service ashore, and transfer orders arrived in New London assigning him to the Bureau of Construction and Repair in Washington. Still upset by the strange silence surrounding the bell, he couldn't help wondering if there was any connection. But when he reported for duty not a word was said about it. His post was in the submarine section. His first day he was busy getting through the formalities. In the late afternoon, however, he had a chance to riffle idly through a pile of "awaiting action" papers his predecessor had left behind.

As he did, he suddenly shook his head in dazed disbelief. There, in the bottom of the basket, pigeonholed for over a year now, was his proposed diving-bell design, King's endorsement, the whole works, just the way it had been sent down from New London.

Momsen didn't trust himself to speak. A trembling despair welled up within him as he thought of the S-51 and Haselden, of her dead captain, Rodney Dobson, of all the wasted months of worry and waiting. He numbly read over his paper, barely able to make out the words. He really didn't have to; he knew them all by heart. Then he sat there wondering what he ought to do. He was too angry to think of anything.

That night he pulled himself together. And in the morning, as diplomatically as possible, he started pleading his case through the bureau. The response was frigid. Who the hell was this new lieutenant? Only two days on the job—word went over the grapevine—and already he was trying to ram through some screwball idea to get people out of submarines. It was his own idea, to boot. You'd think he was the first person who ever thought about it. Why, the bureau had been fooling around with the problem for years.

Momsen persisted nonetheless. But it was no use. The entire plan was dumped back on his desk with an anonymous scrawl: "Impractical from the standpoint of seamanship." Even this he furiously protested. Problems of seamanship were not the bureau's concern at all. Its function, he argued, was to test such schemes for technical feasibility; nobody had yet given him an answer on that count. But the matter, he was huffily informed, was closed. As just another Navy lieutenant, Momsen had nowhere else to go. He could, of course, chuck his career. By now, however, he had two children as well as a wife to support and no visible skill other than submarine skipper. A friend from his Annapolis days urged him to take it easy. Maybe something would turn up.

It did. Tragically, within weeks after his final turndown, the S-4 went to the bottom. In Washington Momsen sat helplessly reading the grim dispatches as her crew slowly asphyxiated. One of the last messages tapped out by the doomed men was an impossible request: "Please hurry."

The headlines touched off a national uproar. Thousands of letters poured into the Navy Department. Get rid of submarines, some insisted. Others, with suggestions enclosed, demanded that a way be found to save such men. As Navy brass fidgeted, many of the letters—pressing for an investigation, pointing darkly to past neglect—had been forwarded on by Congress. A capricious fate saddled Momsen with the task of answering all the mail. It was almost more than he could bear. All the while he was bound in the bitter knowledge that the bell could have made the difference.

And in the end he was not to be denied. As the indignant letters came across his desk for reply, he began to reconsider another idea he had toyed with briefly during the long wait in New London. It offered a completely fresh approach to the problem and it had one enormous advantage over the bell: no official sanction was needed. So, except for the help of a handful of friends, he tackled it with renewed determination on his own—the designing, the building, the testing. It was a device through which men trapped in a submarine could breathe as they rose to the surface; an applauding world would one day call it the Momsen lung. Nor did he stop there. Riding the crest of his magnificent achievement, he was able to resurrect the old bell plan, this time with the Navy's anxious blessing, and to see it also become a reality.

For forty men aboard the *S-4* they were far too late. But on one or the other hinged all the hopes of those still alive in the bowels of the *Squalus*. To prove them both out Swede Momsen had repeatedly braved the unknown. This was the ultimate judgment. Somebody had once asked him what he most feared should another submarine go down. "That I wouldn't be there," he replied.

Now he would be. In Washington, after the terse phone call from the Navy Department, he prepared his departure in ten methodical minutes. Limited to three men on the first flight out, he picked the two doctors attached to his experimental unit along with his most experienced diver. He put the rest of his unit on standby alert and ordered a careful watch kept on the man still in the big pressure tank; this would complete a critical stage in his tests with the helium and oxygen mixtures and he didn't want anything gumming up the works at the last minute. Next he got in touch with his wife, told her what had happened and then tele-phoned a neighbor to look in on her. He even remembered to have his car garaged. He left nothing unfinished, in fact, except the ham sandwich he was eating when his call came.

3

ON THE DARK FLOOR OF THE NORTH ATLANTIC, 243 FEET down, the *Squalus* lay silent. When all of her lights went out, just as she settled on the bottom after her nightmarish descent, the sudden pitch-blackness left each man profoundly alone. And in that desolate instant the enormity of what had happened to them hit home at last. But there was no panic. In a matter of seconds the discipline of their service asserted itself. Beams from a half-dozen flashlights swept through the control room and at a command from Lieutenant Naquin three of the big hand lanterns the *Squalus* carried on board were fished from their storage racks. They cast a ghostly glow.

The light, dim as it was, at least linked the men together again. For a moment they stared uncertainly at one another and then every eye instinctively fastened on the drawn face of Yeoman Charles Kuney, still manning the battle phone, the last terrible scream to surface from one of the after compartments ringing in his ears. Naquin quickly asked him, "Any word aft?" Kuney, his voice a bare whisper, replied, "No, sir."

Naquin quickly took the phone himself. The after battery, he knew, was flooded; the water there was already past the eyeport in the steel door Lloyd Maness had swung shut not more than a minute before. But there were other compartments farther back and it was unthinkable that they had all suffered the same fate. First he tried the forward engine room, then the after engine room. He got no response. That left the after torpedo room. If any of the men back there had managed to escape the savage thrust of the sea, they could be nowhere else. Naquin said with immense care, "Hello, after torpedo room. Can you hear me?" He paused. "Hello," he said. "This is the Captain. *Hello!*" Still there was no answer.

Naquin refused to give up hope. After all, the circuits might be dead. But when he tried the forward battery and the forward torpedo room, each promptly replied. From the forward torpedo room Lieutenant (j.g.) John Nichols added a brave note. "We're okay," Nichols said.

So that was it. Of the seven compartments which divided the *Squalus,* the three forward ones seemed secure for the time being at least; the four after compartments, by every available yardstick, were flooded. The paramount thing now was to get help—in a hurry. And Naquin's first thought rose to the brace of lobster boats he had viewed so nonchalantly from the bridge on the way out; right now they were his only means of sending word of their plight back to the Portsmouth Navy Yard. He immediately instructed Gunner's Mate First Class Eugene Cravens to fire a red smoke rocket, the submariner's disaster signal.

The rockets were in a canister in the control room and Cravens tried desperately to pry open its suddenly stubborn lid. At first he thought it was his own ineptitude. But the sea spilling into the after compartments had displaced so much air forward that the pressure in the control room was nearly double its normal level. Finally Cravens got the lid off, inserted one of the rockets in its cylindrical ejector and launched it toward the surface. After it broke through the waves, it would arch skyward for another eighty feet or so and burst in a reddening cloud of distress.

But it was all in vain. For lobstermen in those waters the comings and goings of submarines were commonplace. Nobody on board either of the two boats had spared the *Squalus* a backward glance and, heading home now against the rising whitecaps, none of them ever gave her a second thought.

In the control room, as soon as Cravens had fired the rocket, Naquin reached Nichols over the battle phone. "John," he said, "release your marker buoy." The bright yellow buoy, some three feet across, nestled flush on the main deck directly above the forward torpedo room. A connecting cable, with a telephone line inside, held it in place on the surface. It was a dramatic moment. Although the buoy had become standard underseas rescue equipment after the development of Swede Momsen's escape lung and his diving bell, it was being used for the first time with the lives of men in the balance. The message on its topside told the whole story: "Submarine Sunk Here. Telephone Inside."

After the marker buoy had been released, Naquin faced a joyless task. During these first minutes on the bottom he had no idea how many men had survived the murderous surge of the sea into his stricken ship. Now he ordered Quartermaster First Class Francis Murphy to muster the crew. The names of those holed up in the forward torpedo room and the forward battery were relayed to Murphy over the battle phone. In the dim lantern light of the control room he continued his grim count. When he had finished, Naquin's worst fears were realized. Of the fifty-nine men on board that morning, only thirty-three could now be accounted for.

In the hush that followed, everyone forgot about the relentless pressure of the North Atlantic backed up inside the maze of pipe and tubing that snaked the length of the *Squalus*. They got a nasty reminder. There was a soft gurgle and suddenly oil spurted all over the control room. Right after it came a wicked geyser of salt water. Ironically, the last man to flee from the after battery, William Isaacs, caught the full force of this new onslaught. Isaacs, who had been placidly preparing meat balls for the noon meal when the dive began, was knocked flat. He tried to scramble up but he was unable to get his footing in the slick oil. More oil covered his face and he could not see. Isaacs was sure that he was going to die. Just then he felt somebody yank him upright.

A moment later the trouble was located; one of the main valves in the hydraulic system overhead had collapsed. Almost before Naquin could give the order, every secondary valve in the system was being frantically turned down. Finally the flow was throttled. Because of the slight upward slant of the *Squalus* on the ocean floor, most of the oil and water had run to the after part of the control room, where it was over a foot deep.

While the men set themselves to mopping up the mess as best they could, Naquin, still hopeful that one of the lobster boats had seen his first distress signal, directed Cravens to send up a second rocket. It was 9:05 A.M. Not quite twenty minutes had elapsed since the most modern submarine in the U.S. Navy had been transformed into a helpless hulk. For some she was already a tomb.

Harold Preble, the naval architect who had been so amazed at the hitchless way the *Squalus* was shaking down, tried to buck up everyone's spirits. He recalled how swiftly Admiral Cole, the Portsmouth Commandant, had reacted when the submarine *Pollack* failed to report surfacing on schedule after a routine dive a few months earlier. The *Pollack* had submerged with a valve that closed the hull aperture for her radio antenna still partially open. While the matter was promptly remedied, her radio had been temporarily knocked out of commission. But Cole, fearing the worst, at once ordered a sister submarine, the *Pike,* to see what was up. "We'll be out of here in no time at all," Preble said. "Four or five hours at most."

No sooner had he finished than more trouble threatened. During the dive Machinist's Mate Second Class Carlton Powell had been assigned to the pump room, directly below the control room. True to his training, Powell had stayed put throughout the dreadful plunge. And now, as he checked to make certain that the suction and discharge valves on the pumps were holding fast, his flashlight picked up a telltale bubbling in the bilge by the bulkhead separating the pump room from the flooded after battery. But Powell could not pinpoint the leak. The news brought Naquin to the pump-room hatch on the double. An anxious inspection, however, revealed that the leak did not seem to be building up any appreciable speed, so he gave instructions to have it watched closely and told Powell to come up into the control room.

Given this breather, Naquin began to consider an intriguing possibility. A number of secondary ballast tanks lining the underbelly of the *Squalus* were still filled with water, including the after trim tank that held her stern on an even keel when she cruised beneath the surface. What if they blew all those tanks?

Naquin quietly talked it over with his executive officer, Walter Doyle. Doyle agreed that it just might work. So he and Lieutenant (j.g.) Robert Robertson, the young navigation officer on board, drove home a lever sending compressed air into the after trim tank. Robertson was sure he felt the *Squalus* respond slightly. But when they looked at her depth and trim indicators, there was no change. Naquin told them to try the auxiliary tanks farther forward. Then he abruptly reversed himself. Even if they were successful, the odds were that this would simply result in increasing the upward angle of the *Squalus,* making it that much more difficult for the diving bell to latch onto the escape hatch over the forward torpedo room.

And Naquin was counting on the bell to get them out. Although there were sufficient Momsen lungs for all hands, he had decided to fall back on them only as a last resort. He was afraid that at this depth in the near-freezing North Atlantic some of his men might lose their hold on the ascending line and shoot to the surface already in the agonizing grip of the bends.

He had kept mum about the lobstermen and his hope that at least one of them would spot his distress signals. But not one beat of a propeller announcing the approach of a ship on the surface had been heard. Naquin now had to face up to the fact that the rockets had gone unseen and with them any chance of triggering a quick rescue operation. That was the worst part; not only were they fearfully far down, each passing minute pinned to the bottom heightening their peril, but nobody knew about it.

The *Squalus* was due to surface at 9:40 A.M. Until then no one at the Portsmouth Navy Yard could possibly have any reason to miss them. Naquin prayed silently that the man on radio duty at Portsmouth this morning was the worrisome sort. But even with the best of luck it would be at least an hour before a major alarm was sounded. As everyone huddled soberly around him, Naquin resigned himself to the inevitable. They were just going to have to sweat it out.

In his precise, no-nonsense manner he said: "You all know where we are. The boat cannot surface by herself. We have released the forward marker buoy and we will continue to send up smoke rockets at regular intervals. It is only a matter of time before help comes. All hands are to be commended on their conduct. I expect no change." He paused. Then, before he could go on, Yeoman Kuney at the battle phone broke in: "Sir, it's Chief Gainor in the forward battery. He says it's urgent."

It was. Gainor, by disconnecting the forward batteries when they started to short on the way down, had staved off an explosion that would have split the hull of the *Squalus* wide open. But this forewarned of a new danger as deadly as drowning—and infinitely more sinister. If salt water seeped into the dry battery cells, the resulting chemical combination would gradually fill the whole compartment with chlorine gas. Now Gainor reported that the water was there. Naquin decided to clear the forward battery at once. Gainor and the five men with him were instructed to take blankets from the quarters where the *Squalus* officers normally slept, strip the pantry of all the tinned goods they could find and move into the forward torpedo room. At the same time Naquin ordered the watertight door on the control-room side of the forward battery opened long enough to bring blankets and mattresses in there. He also had Momsen lungs passed back from the forward torpedo room; in a pinch they could serve as gas masks.

One other problem was resolved. Of the thirty-three men on board still known to be alive, ten were now in the forward torpedo room. The rest were jammed into the control room. To ease the crush Naquin sent five more men up ahead, among them Harold Preble. If and when rescue came, it would be through the escape hatch in the forward torpedo room. Preble, although he probably knew more about submarines than anyone else on board, was technically a civilian and Navy tradition required that he be the first to leave the ship.

Food was for the moment no concern. Besides what had been plucked from the pantry, there was an emergency supply locker in the control room. Each compartment had a ten-gallon container of fresh water as well.

Air, however, was something else again. It was their most

precious—and limited—commodity. To use up as little of it as possible, Naquin forbade any talk unless absolutely necessary and all movement except in the performance of an assigned task. If anyone had to relieve himself, a bucket would be passed periodically. In the control room the men spread oilskin raincoats on the sodden deck and arranged themselves side by side under blankets; some of them had already started to shiver in the cold.

A few minutes later Naquin left on his first inspection tour. He picked his way through the outstretched figures at his feet and, after the door to the forward battery had been swung open, stepped inside the deserted compartment. Guided by his flashlight, he walked forward, stooped to lift the hatch in the passageway and looked down just long enough to see the black water lapping corrosively at the batteries. Next he went into his own tiny stateroom, its unique privacy on the *Squalus* a privileged symbol of his new command. Standing there, Oliver Naquin had never felt more alone.

He reached impulsively into a drawer, took out a small framed photograph of his wife, Frances, and their two children—a girl, nine, and a boy, four—and shoved it into his jacket pocket. As he was about to go, he noticed that his desk chair had tumbled over in one corner. He put it carefully back in place before heading into the forward torpedo room.

It was colder there than in the control room—where the *Squalus* was protected by a double hull—but practically no water had come in. And there were also the ten collapsible bunks, five on each side, in which part of the crew regularly made do. The men who had taken refuge in them looked up expectantly at Naquin's arrival. But there was pathetically little he could say. "We should be getting help soon," he told them. "You must stay quiet. Don't talk. Try to sleep as much as possible."

Afterward he drew junior lieutenant Nichols aside. While

Naquin could only guess at the cause of their plight, he was reasonably sure that the big induction valve high up in the conning tower—the one that funneled air to her surface diesels—had not closed when the *Squalus* went under; there simply was no other explanation for the way the sea poured in as swiftly as it had. So he said to Nichols, "Buzz me as soon as anyone makes contact. Tell them I think the high induction is open. Also that the after battery and both engine rooms are flooded. Say we're not certain about the after torpedo room." As Naquin turned to leave, he stopped and added, "John, there's one more thing. You're doing just fine."

Young Nichols, only three years out of submarine school, was deeply touched. All he could manage in reply was "Thank you, sir." As he watched Naquin depart, he suddenly struck by the awesome load his commanding officer had to carry. It was something nobody else on board could really share and Nichols, even though he was trapped at a depth from which no submariner had ever escaped before, still found himself able to give thanks that he was not in Naquin's shoes.

By the time Naquin returned to the control room, the *Squalus* had completed her first hour on the bottom. To husband what limited light they had, he ordered two of the three hand lanterns switched off. Then he sat down with the others. Like them, all he could do now was wait. But he remained confident that once he failed to report surfacing on schedule, the whole elaborate rescue system that had been devised since the *S-51* and *S-4* disasters would see them safely out. After all the most critical factor—locating the *Squalus*—would be no problem. She had notified Portsmouth as soon as she moved into her diving area, and her diving plans, the point of dive, its duration and direction and exact time of submergence had been duly dispatched and acknowledged.

With such precise navigational aids, Naquin had every reason to believe that only a blind man could miss the marker buoy bobbing in the swells overhead. He had no way of knowing that it would not be quite so simple, that on this morning of all mornings a sheet of paper being routinely bucked through the Portsmouth chain of command had the diving point of the *Squalus* incorrectly recorded.

What now haunted him more than anything else was the memory of those first moments during the dive. Each time Naquin closed his eyes, he saw himself descending from the bridge to the control room, the dive proceeding beautifully, the control board completely green, the *Squalus* unquestionably secure. Only she was not and now, unless a few of them had somehow survived, twenty-six men lay dead in her after compartments. Again and again the green control board came back to blink mockingly at him.

At 10:07 A.M. the *Squalus* sent her third smoke rocket aloft. Naquin knew this was pushing things—Portsmouth could hardly be expected to react that quickly—but the thought that some sort of ship might be in the neighborhood was irresistible. At 10:24 a fourth rocket was fired; Quartermaster Murphy, keeping the log, gravely marked the time.

In the forward torpedo room they could hear it swirl up. Nichols had just finished tutoring Preble in the use of a Momsen lung if it came to that. "Above all else," Nichols warned, "hang on to the ascending line." But even this would not make much difference unless somebody was standing by to fish them out. Although the lung could be converted into a makeshift float once you reached the surface, it was no buffer against the icy North Atlantic.

Such odd goings on continued to mystify one of the two Filipino mess attendants on board, Feliciano Elvina. Camped now in the forward torpedo room next to his countryman Basilio

Galvan, he tried again to find out what this was all about. Galvan, although he had begun to suspect that there was more to it than he first imagined, was still not sure. But he had once served in a submarine that had been used in a simulated rescue with Momsen's diving bell, so in an effort to save face he replied in Spanish, "It is nothing. Simply a practice." By then their agitated exchange reached Nichols and he ordered them to pipe down. Elvina, however, was unable to contain himself any longer. He indignantly declared, "Basilio say this a practice. I say this no damn practice." Nichols couldn't believe his ears. Then he started to laugh; it was the only occasion for laughter he would have this May 23rd.

Naquin in the control room overheard a different kind of talk. For the first time someone was discussing the fate of the men who had been caught in the after compartments. Nothing could lower morale faster and he broke in with a sharp edge to his voice. "There will be no more of that!" he snapped.

But not mentioning them was one thing; to stop thinking about them was quite another. And for affable Lloyd Maness, out of North Carolina's hill country, it was hardest of all. In case anything went wrong, his job was to close the watertight door between the control room and the after battery no matter who was on the other side. It had been drilled into him repeatedly and his response to the sudden flooding of the engine rooms was automatic. But nobody ever told Maness how he was supposed to feel afterward.

Even though he had held the door open long enough for six men to scramble to safety, he could think only about those who had not made it. In his private torment, the same question kept coming back to him. How many of them had been stumbling forward in the darkness, frantically calling to him to hold the door open just a few more seconds, their voices lost in the roar of the surging water? Then he thought of something else. Because of the rotation of the crew during these trial runs he would have been back there himself for the afternoon dive. As he sat hunched over on the control-room deck he chewed savagely on a clenched fist and it took him a long time to realize that the funny taste in his mouth was blood.

Like Maness, fully a third of the men forward would have pulled duty in the after compartments that afternoon. Each in his own way considered the irony of their deliverance. It never occurred to any of them that those who had died swiftly in the first rush of the sea might be the lucky ones; just being alive was all that counted.

For Torpedoman Third Class Leonard de Medeiros, the whole business still seemed unreal. De Medeiros had been born and raised in New Bedford, Massachusetts. He was no different from any other submariner and never completely discounted the possibility of ending up like this. But he always figured that if it happened, it would be in some remote corner of the world and not practically over the horizon from the beaches where he had swum as a boy. De Medeiros was standing watch on the marker-buoy telephone. Once again, when the fourth rocket was launched, he instinctively clapped the headset tighter around his ears. All he heard was the steady slap of the waves against the buoy.

Huddled in a nearby bunk, William Isaacs, drenched and oil-smeared, suddenly remembered that when he relieved breakfast cook Robert Thompson in the galley, Thompson had told him that he was going to nap during the dive. Isaacs himself had often done the same thing and he wondered if Thompson woke up in time to realize what was going on. The thought of dying like that horrified him and he tried to pray for the salvation of Thompson and the others. But he was shivering so from the wet and cold that he could not form the words. The best he could manage was a mumbled hope that their souls might "rest in peace."

Chief Torpedoman Roy Campbell dwelt with equal chagrin on a less spiritual matter. Just the night before he had finally gotten around to describing the delights of life aboard the *Squalus* in a letter to a buddy he had served with in one of the Navy's vintage *S* boats. Campbell couldn't resist rubbing it in. "Better put in for a transfer," he postscripted, "before they retire you, too!" Afterward he stamped and addressed the envelope and slipped it into a hip pocket of his dungarees. The letter was still there and on second thought he decided that maybe mailing it was not such a good idea after all.

At least one man, Machinist's Mate Second Class Carol Pierce, was certain of eventual rescue. He looked at it this way. If it were not for an errant softball, he would have been in the flooded after engine room right now. But in a game played over the weekend at Portsmouth a member of the crew had been conked on the head by a wild pitch and was left behind in the hospital with a possible concussion. In the juggling of assignments that followed, Pierce wound up manning the air-pressure levers in the control room this morning. With that sort of thing going for him, he figured he was rolling a hot pair of dice.

In the control room, meanwhile, Naquin wrestled with a new problem. After the initial rocket firings failed to produce any results, he made up his mind to hold off launching more of them until Portsmouth had time to swing into action. But it was now well past eleven o'clock and there was still no sign of the search operation he had expected to materialize overhead. He knew there was one variable that could gum up everything at this point—the weather. Although it was late in the season for one of those three-day blows out of the northeast that periodically lash the New England coast, he remembered how much the wind had started kicking up the sea just before he left the bridge. With an effort he forced such conjecture aside; whatever it was like on the surface, there was absolutely nothing he could do about it.

Then, at the suggestion of Executive Officer Walter Doyle, a new tack was taken to help search ships zero in on them. Doyle handled it himself. He grabbed a can of oil, sloshed his way through the water at the after end of the control room and dumped it into the crew's toilet. With any luck, once he flushed the oil out, it would rise in a billowing stain around the marker buoy. Naquin gave it twenty minutes before ordering Gunner's Mate First Class Cravens to send up his fifth smoke rocket.

As it left the ejector, Cravens whispered, "Go baby, go!" He spoke for them all. Somehow, without a word being exchanged, everyone grew tensely expectant; this was the big one.

But nothing happened. And as the trapped crewmen slowly settled back they continued to remain remarkably disciplined despite the colossal disaster that had befallen them; now, however, there was a new note of resignation about it. To divert them as much as anything, Naquin directed both compartments to chow down. Almost everybody ignored the canned beans on hand in favor of tins of peaches and pineapple. The fruit, especially the pineapple, made them feel warmer.

At 12:40 P.M. a sixth rocket was fired. Exactly four hours had passed since the *Squalus* had dipped beneath the surface. In the control room one of the men asked Naquin, "Sir, when will we be rescued?"

At the Portsmouth Navy Yard that morning Rear Admiral Cyrus Cole nodded briskly to a Marine Corps orderly and entered his office just after 8:30. He was a peppery little man with an imposing head and a piercing gaze that made him seem larger than he actually was. Nearing the end of a long and distinguished career, he would be retired from active duty a year hence. And although not a submariner himself he had a special affinity for the men who manned the Navy's "pigboats." His only son was then serving aboard one in the Pacific, and prior to coming to Portsmouth Cole had spent two years commanding the Submarine Force, U.S. Fleet. Now, as he liked to wisecrack, "They sent me back to see how they're built."

A relatively routine day loomed ahead. Along with the normal construction and repair work at the yard, just two ships in his care would be at sea. Besides the *Squalus* out on her trial runs, the *Sculpin* was to depart later in the morning on a two-month shakedown cruise to South America. The only thing out of the ordinary was a party of political V.I.P.s scheduled to show up at noon. The V.I.P. visit had forced Cole's industrial manager at the yard, Captain Halford Greenlee, to cancel his plans to drive down to the overnight anchorage of the *Squalus* and sail with her today. Greenlee had been especially looking forward to the trip; her engineering officer, Ensign Joseph Patterson, was his son-in-law.

Now, as Greenlee and other members of the yard staff arrived to go over the tour arranged for the rubbernecking politicos, Cole's chief clerk handed him a transcript of the last message from the *Squalus* noting the time, place and course of her dive. Cole glanced at it and then, putting it aside, remarked to Captain Greenlee, "Sorry you couldn't go out with her today." Greenlee would remember his answer as long as he lived. "It's nothing," he said. "I can always catch her another time."

When the *Squalus* failed to report surfacing promptly at 9:40 that morning, nobody at Portsmouth gave it much thought. It would not be the first time a submarine had been tardy on that score and Cole, having dismissed his staff, continued to work his way through the morning mail stacked on his desk. But then the minutes stretched into an hour. Cole called in his aide, Lieutenant Commander John Curley. "Why haven't we heard from the *Squalus* yet?" he demanded. Curley, who was soon to ship out for some sea duty and had been busy breaking in an officer assigned to succeed him, replied, "I don't know, sir. I was just about to call it to your attention. I'm getting a little concerned." "So am I," Cole said. "It's probably an oversight of some sort but check on it right away."

Before Curley could leave Cole's office, the duty officer in the Portsmouth radio room rang up with a report that he had been trying for twenty minutes without success to establish contact with the *Squalus*. Cole directed Curley to telephone the Boston Navy Yard to see if it could raise the missing submarine. When this proved as fruitless, Cole grew increasingly apprehensive. Still it was difficult for him to believe that the worst had happened; he had already had one false alarm this year with the *Pollack*. But then Curley reported that the Coast Guard lookout station on the offshore Isles of Shoals was unable to spot any sign of the *Squalus* either, and Cole could no longer doubt that something was seriously wrong. After a fretful moment he snatched up the last message from the *Squalus* and hurried out of his office.

It was now nearly eleven o'clock, and on the bridge of the *Sculpin* Lieutenant Commander Warren Wilkin surveyed last-minute preparations for her 11:30 departure from Portsmouth. Wilkin was in fine fettle; after months of training and trials, the *Sculpin* was for all practical purposes part of the Navy's fighting fleet. On her way south she would stop off at Newport, Rhode Island, to pick up her live torpedoes and then head for Coco Solo, Panama.

Suddenly Wilkin was astonished to see Admiral Cole striding posthaste toward the *Sculpin*'s berth and barely had time to scramble down to the main deck before Cole came on board. Skipping the amenities, Cole told him, "I want you to shove off immediately. The *Squalus* may be in trouble. We're not sure. Here's her diving point. I want you to pass over it and let me know what you find without delay."

As Wilkin acknowledged the order, Cole was already on his way off the *Sculpin* on a mission as urgent. The Navy at that time had on tap five of the diving bells pioneered by Swede Momsen; now known officially as submarine rescue chambers, the only one close enough to be of help in an emergency was carried by a converted World War I mine sweeper, the *Falcon*. When Cole got back to his office, a quick check of her operating schedule showed that she was then at her home base in New London, Connecticut. Cole promptly put through a call to the Commandant at New London, Captain Richard Edwards, to alert him that the services of the *Falcon* might be needed at a moment's notice.

As luck would have it, Cole's call could not have caught the ancient vessel more ill-prepared—undergoing an annual overhaul. The *Falcon*'s boilers were dead, the big ten-ton rescue chamber had been removed from her squat fantail and most of her crew was ashore on liberty. But Edwards grimly promised to have her under way as soon as possible.

In Portsmouth all Cole could do after that was to sit tight until he received some word from the *Sculpin*. As the minutes dragged by, a sober assemblage of officers gathered in his office, among them Captain Greenlee. Then just before noon, having cleared the mouth of the Piscataqua, the *Sculpin* relayed her first ominous report: "Have not sighted the *Squalus*. Am calling her with sound gear and proceeding to her diving point."

Cole's response was swift. "Inform the *Sculpin*," he ordered, "to remain searching in the area until some trace of the *Squalus* is found." To the officers around him, he added: "Gentlemen, I'm afraid we're in for a very bad time."

Captain Greenlee, his face ashen, excused himself and went into his own office. His daughter Betty and Ensign Patterson—"Pat" as they all called him—had been married for ten months. Only the previous weekend Betty's biggest worry had been whether she and

Pat would be able to spend their first wedding anniversary together before the *Squalus* joined the fleet. Now what was Greenlee to tell her? The young couple had set up housekeeping in an apartment off the base. But after a minute's indecision, fearful of finding his daughter alone, he decided against calling the apartment. Instead he dialed his own house, where his son Bob, an Army lieutenant home on leave, was staying. Young Greenlee's wife, Jacqueline, happened to answer the phone. She still recalls her father-in-law's strained voice.

"Betty isn't there, is she?"

"Why no, Dad," she replied. "Is something wrong?"

"She may be down," Greenlee blurted out.

"What's down? I don't understand."

"Pat's boat, the *Squalus!*"

About that time Lieutenant Naquin's wife, Frances, left their rented house and started driving toward the Portsmouth Navy Yard, unaware that the *Squalus* was long overdue. On the way Mrs. Naquin had one stop to make. She had promised to pick up Betty Patterson. The wives of the *Squalus* officers were throwing a luncheon for the *Sculpin* wives to cheer them up a bit after the departure of their husbands. In the afternoon they would all play bridge together.

When Mrs. Naquin turned into the block where the Pattersons lived, she found Betty standing at the curb with her brother Bob. "Dad wants me over at his place right away," Betty Patterson explained. "Bob won't tell me why." After she had got into her brother's car, Lieutenant Greenlee came around to Mrs. Naquin and said, "You better come, too."

Out in the North Atlantic, misguided by the error in the reported diving position of the *Squalus,* the *Sculpin* circled vainly over the supposed point of submergence. The sea had a cold metallic cast, like pewter, and overhead a fat-bellied bank of gray clouds now completely covered the sky. As the *Sculpin* churned through the swells seeking some sign of her lost sister ship, a half-dozen lookouts on her bridge anxiously scanned the surface; below deck her underwater sound gear continued to ping out the call letters of the *Squalus*.

The *Squalus,* according to the last message recorded at Portsmouth, dived at longitude of 70° 31' W. But, as it turned out, the actual longitude was 70° 36' W. This meant that the *Squalus* had in fact gone down five miles west of where the *Sculpin* was concentrating her search. Even worse, since the *Squalus* was heading southeast at the time of her submergence, every time the *Sculpin* trailed her course on the surface, she moved still farther away from the true position of the sunken submarine.

What caused the mix-up in longitude was never conclusively settled. But the trouble probably lay in the peculiarity of the Morse code symbols for "one" and "six." They are the exact opposite of each other. "One" is formed by a dot and four dashes. "Six" on the other hand is a dash and four dots. Somewhere along the line, either in transmission or reception, they must have been inadvertently switched.

The *Sculpin* might have hunted on endlessly had it not been for a young officer on her wind-blown bridge, Lieutenant (j.g.) Ned Denby. Pausing for an instant to wipe the spray out of his eyes, Denby happened to glance the wrong way at precisely the right moment. Every muscle in his body stiffened. He thought he saw a smudge astern just above the horizon. He blinked once and took another look. The smudge was still there and it seemed to Denby that it could have been made by a smoke bomb.

He shouted out his discovery at once and Lieutenant Commander Wilkin caught a glimpse of the smudge in his binoculars seconds before it disappeared. Wilkin immediately radioed a terse message back to Portsmouth: "Believe sighted smoke bomb." Not a man on her bridge spoke as the *Sculpin* swung around and began backtracking at emergency speed.

Ten minutes after Ensign Denby had made his fateful sighting, the men trapped inside the *Squalus* first heard the sound of the *Sculpin*'s propellers drawing near. What Denby had seen was the sixth rocket fired by the *Squalus* just after her crew had finished their initial meal on the bottom. None of them got very excited. Rather there was a mood of stunned relief. Too many times their hopes had risen with the rockets fired that morning and now nobody was sure that his ears weren't playing some kind of macabre trick. But the propeller beat grew unmistakably louder and at last Lieutenant Naquin sent another rocket up.

It exploded high in the air some three hundred yards in front of the *Sculpin* a little to the starboard. Right after that her lookouts spied the marker buoy riding in the boisterous sea. As the *Sculpin* eased alongside, the buoy was gingerly hauled on deck with boat hooks and one line fastened around a cleat while Warren Wilkin reached inside for the phone. A moment later he said, "Hello, *Squalus*, this is *Sculpin*. What's your trouble?"

In the forward torpedo room of the *Squalus*, 243 feet down, young John Nichols struggled to maintain his composure. Quickly he sketched the flooded condition of the submarine. Then Wilkin heard Nichols say, "Hold the phone. I'll put the Captain on."

There was a pause of about thirty seconds before Oliver Naquin said with quiet elation, "Hello, Wilkie." But just as Wilkin started to respond, the *Sculpin* suddenly rose high on an ocean swell and the line went dead. Snarled on the deck rigging of the *Squalus*, the marker-buoy cable, which was the sole physical link she had with the surface, had parted. Once more she was lost.

4

IN PORTSMOUTH WILKIN'S MESSAGE THAT HE HAD SIGHTED A smoke bomb was all Admiral Cole needed. He grabbed the telephone himself and asked for the Chief of Naval Operations in Washington.

And minutes later the news was being relayed to Navy bases and Coast Guard stations all along the northeast coast that the submarine *Squalus* was missing and presumed on the bottom. Before the day was done the greatest underseas rescue operation in history would be in full swing.

Cole's call earlier in the morning to New London warning that the *Falcon* might be required would save precious hours. Police and shore patrol teams were already out rounding up members of the *Falcon*'s crew on liberty while the skeleton gang on duty in her engine room labored feverishly to get the boilers going. Steam was essential not only to propel her but to run the power winches which would lift the big rescue chamber from the dock back onto her fantail. Without it the *Falcon* was worthless and up on the bridge her freckle-faced young skipper, Lieutenant George Sharp, paced to and fro in furious frustration.

Cole himself prepared to proceed to the scene aboard his old Navy yard tug, the *Penacook*. Just as he was about to embark at 1:20 P.M. a second message came in from the *Sculpin:* "Have sighted marker buoy."

For Cole and the others this was perhaps the worst moment. Up until then, despite their fears, they could still cling to the slender hope that somehow it would all turn out to be a false alarm; now even this vanished.

In Washington the man who meant the difference between life and death for the trapped crew of the *Squalus* hurried on board a waiting twin-engine amphibian at the Anacostia Naval Air Station and disappeared into the haze toward Portsmouth at the best speed the plane could make—150 knots.

Since that one call less than an hour before from Commander Lockwood at the Navy Department, Swede Momsen had received no further word about the *Squalus* prior to taking off. The irony was enormous; for years he had dreaded this day and prepared ceaselessly for it and now that it had come he had no real idea of what he was going up against. Buckled in his seat, all he could do was wonder if he had overlooked something, some secret mockery of the sea reserved especially for him and those who still survived in the *Squalus*. As he would write later of that flight in a letter to his wife, "I never felt more humble. It seemed as if all the gods were pointing at me."

Momsen had good reason to think so. When he first submitted plans for his diving bell after the *S-51* went down, the suggestions being bandied about to get anyone out of a submarine were incredibly primitive. One popular theory held that you could reach the surface with your head inside a bubble of air. Out of curiosity he tried it and discovered to his consternation that the theory had a major defect. The bubble disintegrated on the way up.

Under such circumstances the rude rejection of his bell idea just before the tragic loss of the S-4 very nearly caused Momsen to quit the Navy in disgust. But then a daring new concept—of escape from below rather than rescue from the surface—began to grip his imagination. It centered around the premise that if a man had the physical ability to stand in water up to his chin and breathe, he could also breathe into a bag positioned on his chest at a level corresponding to that of his lungs. Assuming that the air supply was revitalized, Momsen asked himself, why couldn't a man breathe back and forth into the the bag even though his head was underwater?

It sounded logical enough—except that nobody had thought of it before. And whether it would work or not was another matter. To find out, however, one thing was certain: Momsen would not go through official channels again. After his bitter experience with the bell he figured he didn't have any choice. Instead, for the kind of technical help he needed, he approached a clever young engineer in the Bureau of Construction and Repair named Frank Hobson, who specialized in what passed for research and development in those days; better yet, as a civilian Hobson could afford to wink at the Navy's hidebound ways.

Hobson was immediately intrigued by the idea and agreed to comb through his files for anything that might relate to submarine escape. In the end he managed to turn up reports on a number of contraptions, but none of them had really panned out. While each had been introduced with considerable fanfare at one time or another—particularly a model developed in Germany—every device up until then was either too bulky or balky and nowhere had there been any serious effort to train submarine crews in their use.

So there was nothing left for Momsen to do except start from scratch. It was an audacious undertaking, probing an alien world as no man before him had ever done, without funds, operating almost alone, buoyed only by his belief in himself and determined this time not to be thwarted.

His first problem—revitalizing the bag's air supply—proved simple enough; soda lime was already known to be an effective absorbent for carbon dioxide, the poisonous waste product of expired air. But some means had to be found to replenish the amount of oxygen a man would consume during the time it took him to reach the surface. A day's research in a medical library convinced Momsen that a supply of pure oxygen would be needed. Since the body will use only as much oxygen as it requires at any given moment, an amount sufficient to cover the escape period was all he needed. That night Momsen went to bed thinking that he had the whole thing licked.

By morning his restless mind told him he had not. What if the oxygen requirements made the bag too big? The resulting buoyancy would send its hapless user sailing to the surface out of control, his body unable to endure such rapid decompression. Thus, the size of the bag now became the critical factor—and in more ways than one. It had to be of a dimension that a man's lungs could easily handle. It also had to be large enough to supply him with enough oxygen to rise to the surface safely. Finally it had to be small enough to enable him to control his upward movement.

For someone whose formal schooling had shaped him for duty as a line officer in the U.S. Navy, Momsen was getting into pretty deep water. At the time practically nothing was known about the environment a human might encounter in the ocean depths or the mysterious changes it wrought on his body chemistry. But from the beginning Momsen's instinct was to have the bag function like lungs right down to its placement on the chest. Somehow, he sensed, this would keep him on the track.

He was right. The average capacity of human lungs measured in liquid terms turned out to be somewhat more than a gallon, so breathing in and out of a bag that size presented no problem. It was also large enough for the kind of ascents up to 300 feet that Momsen foresaw as submarines increased their test depth. Keying the capacity of the bag to that of real lungs even took care of the danger of going up too fast; it would produce only about eight pounds of buoyancy.

Out of his investigation into previous attempts to engineer escape apparatus, Momsen did learn one vital lesson. They had all been far too complex. But buttressed by Hobson's technical know-how, he finally settled on a design that seemed to fill the bill.

The bag, made of rubber and resembling nothing so much as a hot-water bottle, hung around the neck with additional straps around the waist. A canister of soda lime inside it filtered out the carbon dioxide. Leading to the mouthpiece were two tubes, one to breathe in the oxygen and the other to exhale it. A valve on the bottom side of the bag automatically allowed excess oxygen to escape as the pressure decreased during an ascent. Between the mouthpiece and the tubes there was a second valve which would retain the oxygen still in the bag once the surface was reached, so that it could serve as an emergency life preserver. That, aside from a noseclip, was it.

Building a working model was something else again. To do it Momsen enlisted another confederate, Chief Gunner Clarence Tibbals, who headed up the diving school at the Washington Navy Yard. A salty veteran, Tibbals had won the Navy Cross for the part he played in trying to rescue the crew of the S-4 and it didn't take much to get him to lend his workshop to the project. But latching on to the right materials still stretched everyone's ingenuity to the limit. All the rubber, for example, was eventually scrounged from old inner tubes. This accounted for the large red patch that decorated Momsen's first artificial lung.

Little more than a month after he had committed himself to its development—on February 25, 1928—the lung was ready for testing in the model boat basin at the yard. The officer in charge, in giving Momsen permission to ignore the "POSITIVELY NO SWIMMING" sign afterhours, dryly noted, "Swede, if your heart's desire is to emulate a fish, who am I stand in your way? Only do me a favor and don't drown. It won't look good on my record."

Momsen cut a memorable figure in his woolen tank suit, the rubber bag with its red patch drooping around his neck, a clothespin serving as his noseclip. He entered the basin at its shallow end and walked slowly down the incline until the water was just below his eyes. He stood there breathing in and out of the bag for thirty seconds or so. Then, gravely saluting Hobson and Tibbals, he took a final step and went in over his head. That first trial lasted less than three minutes, but for submariners everywhere it was the beginning of a new era.

Night after night Momsen returned to the basin, drifting around its bottom at a depth of ten feet, weighed down by a hunk of scrap iron, his imagination carrying him through all the compartments of a submarine pinned helplessly on the ocean floor.

Three weeks later he was ready to switch to a pressure tank at the yard that was used by Tibbals and his divers to simulate conditions in the sea. When the tank was partially filled with water, compressed air was admitted to build the pressure to any desired depth, starting off at fifty feet. Momsen described his first experience in the tank in a letter to a friend:

There was the hiss of the air and then the intense heat caused by the added pressure. Suddenly the pressure on my ears became almost unbearable and I held my nose and blew as hard as I could. At fifty feet I filled the bag with oxygen and ducked down under the water holding a line attached to an anchor. Tibbals was peering intently through the eyeport watching every move I made from his control station outside the tank. I waved my hand and he threw open the exhaust valve allowing the pressure to fall at a rate approximately equal to the change of pressure that would have taken place had I been rising through the water. While I actually did not move, I had the sensation of surfacing. The bag swelled as the pressure fell and the excess gas escaped through a valve in the bottom just as we planned.

From fifty feet in the pressure tank, Momsen gradually worked his way down to a simulated hundred feet, then to 150, 200, 250 and finally to 300 feet. While several of the divers under Tibbals had joined in the experiments by then, Momsen was always the first one to try each new test. He considered himself responsible for any mishap that might occur as he pushed farther into the unknown, and although everything had gone off without a hitch so far, he could never quite rid himself of the feeling that a hidden danger lurked somewhere in all of this.

Once his trials in the pressure tank were finished, he faced an odd paradox. Before he could attempt a real ascent, he had to have some means of getting down deep enough in the water to do it. Tibbals supplied the solution. He had listened to Momsen talk about his old diving-bell plan and decided to adapt some of its features. In this instance the "bell" was fashioned from half of a pickle barrel requisitioned from the enlisted men's mess. Two vertical boards were nailed to its open end and connected with a crosspiece. After the whole contrivance was weighted and in the water, Momsen could stand on the crosspiece with his head and shoulders inside the barrel and breathe the air that had been trapped there. A hose from the surface kept the air supply renewed while a manila line regulated the barrel's movement. When it reached a predetermined depth, all Momsen had to do was slip outside and glide back up.

He decided to baptize the pickle barrel in a tank some sixty feet deep which was normally reserved for testing mines. Getting into such depths, without any of the control factors of the pressure tank, added a new wrinkle to the lung's basic equipment—an ascending line that ran up to a wooden buoy on the surface. Along this line he strung a number of cork "stop" marks; at each stop there would be a pause, measured by a prescribed number of breaths, so that a man coming up could safely decompress. Although Momsen's first ascent from the pickle barrel was a cautious twenty feet, rising the mine tank's full sixty feet was routine by the advent of summer. The same exhilarating thought swept over him each time he did it. If he had been on the bottom in a submarine and had some way of getting out, he would have been able to reach the surface safely.

While word had circulated that Momsen was fiddling around with some sort of escape device, nobody had taken it very seriously. The best engineering minds in the country, after all, had been called in following the S-4 tragedy and nothing was off the drawing board yet. Now, he decided, the moment had come for a dramatic demonstration of what the lung could do and he searched through charts of the Potomac River until he located a hole 110 feet deep off Morgantown, Maryland.

Since the pickle barrel could not stand up under the downstream tides of the Potomac, a similar contraption of steel had been put together and was brought to the Morgantown hole on board the little diving boat *Crilley*. But the river was still ebbing so fast on the morning of their arrival that Momsen had to wait for slack water. This didn't leave much margin for error, and as soon as the current subsided, the new rig was lowered into the Potomac. It was really nothing more than a steel box three feet by four feet and thirty inches high; like its rickety predecessor, there was also a platform underneath its open bottom.

Even though the sun was almost at its zenith as Momsen started down, the muddy Potomac turned absolutely black before he had gone twenty feet. As he continued his descent, he could feel the sharp pain behind his ears as the pressure mounted to more than four times what it had been on the surface. Just when he was wondering if the trip would ever end, the platform touched down with a slight bump and suddenly began to settle in the slimy river bed. For a panicky second it seemed as if he would be buried in it. But the loathsome ooze stopped just short of his knees. Worse yet was the stench that accompanied it. Momsen couldn't wait to inflate his lung from a flask of pressurized oxygen and put on his noseclip.

After the buoy had been released that would bring the ascending line to the surface, Momsen tested his lung. The usually faint clicking noises of its valves magnified eerily in the stillness of the steel box. Once his breathing had assumed its normal rhythm, he crouched down in the muck to get outside for his ascent. As he did, his fingers brushed against a rock and he impulsively stuck it into the top of his tank suit. When he was a boy, the way to prove you could dive to the bottom of the local swimming hole was to come up with a fistful of pebbles; the temptation to pull the same sort of stunt now was too much to resist.

Momsen used both his hands and his feet on the line to control his speed. This was a far cry from the clear waters of the mine tank and he fought against the urge to go faster. Finally the color of the river changed to a deep chocolate that gradually grew lighter until all at once he found himself staring up into the brilliant blue sky he had left some ten minutes before. He held up the rock he had brought with him just long enough for everyone to have a good look and then tossed it nonchalantly over his head back into the Potomac. It was a moment nobody there would ever forget. The 110 feet Swede Momsen had risen was precisely the depth at which the *S-4* had been lost.

Everything went so smoothly that three of the divers who had been working with him were able to make successful ascents before the tide rolled in again. A huge grin creased Momsen's face as a triumphant broom was lashed to the *Crilley's* mast—it had been a clean sweep.

The Navy found out what had happened off Morgantown exactly like everyone else—by reading the papers. Midway through the testing, someone who looked like a high school kid on the riverbank started waving and shouting so persistently that Momsen finally sent a dory over to him. He turned out to be a cub reporter for the Washington *Star* named A. W. Gilliam. After being allowed to experience the sensations of an ascent from twenty feet, Gilliam raced back to his office with the scoop of a lifetime. The next day, when the *Crilley* returned to Washington, a notable collection of brass, including some with rather red faces, was on hand to greet her; among those present was the Chief of Naval Operations himself, Admiral Charles Hughes, who spoke for them all when he demanded of Momsen, "Young man, what the hell have you been up to?"

The news made headlines across the nation and the Navy, of course, quickly approved more tests. Momsen chose to conduct them in the Chesapeake Bay in 155 feet of water—deeper by four fathoms than the *S-51* had been on the morning he found the oil slick where she had finally come to rest. A bigger base ship was required for a location as exposed to the weather as this, and the *Falcon*—the same ship now frantically getting up steam to go to the aid of the *Squalus*—was dispatched from New London. She was an especially appropriate choice; from her decks had come not only the futile attempts to save the men trapped in the *S-51* but those in the S-4 as well. Veterans of both disasters still served with her, and Momsen was deeply moved on the eve of his first ascent in the Chesapeake when a group of them came to him. "Sir," a spokesman said, "We just want you to know that we are proud to have you on board."

As a precautionary measure so far down, Momsen decided to run a safety line around his waist up to the surface. He thought it might make all the difference in case something went wrong. It would, instead, nearly cost him his life.

Because of some minor technical delays he was not lowered into the great bay until late in the afternoon, and by the time he had adjusted his lung and was ready to come back up, it was as dark as it had been in the Potomac. He had risen about fifty feet when he was suddenly stopped short. It took him a moment to realize what had happened. His safety line had unaccountably gone taut; what's more, it was leading straight down.

After a couple of experimental tugs he concluded that it must somehow have become tangled in his diving rig. He first tried to see if he could worm out of it with one hand while he held on to the ascending line with the other. When this didn't work, he considered yanking on the safety line in an effort to free it. But the men tending the line on the surface might mistake it for a signal to haul him up. If they did, they would simply be dragging him back down, fouling the line further or, even worse, pinning him against the steel box he had just left.

He could think of only one thing to do: crawl down the ascending line and try to find where the safety line had snagged. This, however, raised a chilling prospect. For Momsen time was beginning to run out; he had already used part of his precious oxygen and the increased pressure he would encounter going down might force so much more of it from the lung that he would not have enough for the return trip up.

But he had no alternative and down he went, blindly groping his way along, the murky depths of the bay relentlessly closing in around him. It was, as it turned out, exactly the right move to make. When he reached the bottom, he drew in the safety line and discovered that it had caught on a corner of the platform where he stood during his descent. He cleared it with a flick of his wrist and started up again. After he got to the surface and was hustled on board the *Falcon,* they examined his lung. It had barely enough oxygen in it for two more minutes—about thirty breaths.

The fault, however, had not been with the lung itself and for Momsen that was all that counted. Subsequent trials in the Chesapeake went off without difficulty and upon their completion he prepared for an exploit beyond anything he had thus far attempted. The one element lacking in all his previous tests with the lung had been a submarine. That would soon be remedied.

Salvaged some three months after she had become a coffin for her crew of forty, the *S-4* had been rusting away ever since at the Boston Navy Yard. At first there were vague plans to put her back into service, but they had never progressed very far. Then Momsen learned that she was going to be sold for scrap and promptly badgered his superiors to turn the *S-4* over to him as a test ship for submarine safety. What he planned was to allow himself to be purposely trapped inside her. He was motivated by something more than sheer bravado. As he noted, "Telling some poor submariner that he can come up through a hundred feet of water isn't going to mean much unless he can get out to do it in the first place."

Momsen personally directed the *S-4*'s conversion. She was given no power of her own; instead she would be towed wherever she was needed. Of the five compartments submarines of her class carried, the control room and battery were reconditioned to house her test crew. The other three compartments—torpedo room, engine room and motor room—would be reserved for experimental flooding and escape.

The means of escape were artfully contrived. Around a hatch in the motor room, Momsen installed a steel "skirt" extending down into the compartment about four feet. The idea was to get the crew out of a stricken submarine by first unlocking the hatch cover and then letting the sea in through the compartment's flood valves. As the water came in, it would compress the air in the compartment until the hatch was forced open. After the water level rose above the lower edge of the skirt, the external and internal pressure would equalize, leaving an air pocket at the top of the compartment where the men could don their lungs before rising to the surface through the hatch.

Momsen hooked up a similar skirt in the torpedo room, the only difference being that the hatchway, used to load torpedoes, was slightly angled. But in the engine room he tried another scheme. It was a cylindrical "escape lock" built above the hatch which could hold four men at a time. It worked on exactly the same principles of pressure, except that only the lock rather than the whole compartment had to be flooded.

There was, however, a rub to all of this. Nobody could be absolutely certain that enough air would remain in either compartment or the lock to support life after it was flooded. It boiled down to this: Momsen was going to have to find out the hard way.

The resurrected hulk of the S-4 once again went to the bottom on February 6, 1929, off Key West, Florida. A small flotilla of attending craft hovered on the surface as Momsen and Edward Kalinoski, a skinny chief torpedoman from Jersey City who had participated in the first ascents in the Potomac, rode in the S-4's control room with her caretaker crew. But once they touched down at forty feet the two men went into the motor room and shut themselves in. Kalinoski unlocked the hatch overhead and a moment later Momsen opened the flood valves. The water flowed quickly across the deck; as they watched, it crept past their knees and began licking at their waists. "Mr. Momsen," said Kalinoski, "I hope to Christ you know what you're doing."

Short of an actual disaster, they could not have more closely duplicated conditions that had taken an endless procession of lives. The pressure continued to build up inside the motor room. Suddenly there was an enormous crash as the hatch flew open and the sea started pouring in. Every few seconds there was an angry interruption as great bubbles of air fought their way through the hatch. The water level in the compartment shot up at a fearsome rate until it rose over the edge of the steel skirt—and just below their chins. Once that happened, no more air escaped and thus no more water came in. Everything fell quiet; the water, which had been surging up so furiously seconds ago, lapped peacefully against the compartment bulkheads. It had gone precisely as Momsen thought it would.

Kalinoski took the ascending line, tied one end of it to a cleat on the skirt and sent the other end with its wooden buoy floating to the surface. Then he and Momsen inflated their lungs. Momsen was the first to leave. He ducked into the water, went up through the skirt out of the hatch and waited for Kalinoski to appear. Compared to previous ascents in the Potomac and the Chesapeake, it was easy going in water as clear and warm as this, but there was a big difference. Only fourteen months before, eight men had perished without a chance in the same motor room from which they had just emerged so effortlessly.

Although he was soon escaping at a hundred feet, which was as far down as his orders called for with the S-4, boats of her class had been designed to dive to two hundred feet and Momsen was anxious to come up from that depth as well. This caused quite a flap since the Navy, by now basking in world praise and as skittish over the possibility of something going wrong as it had once been skeptical of the lung having any value at all, was reluctant to risk it. But the knowledge that such an escape had actually taken place, Momsen argued, would be a huge psychological boost for every submariner who had to learn to use the lung.

The historic trip measured exactly 207 feet and the memory of it would linger with Momsen always. No man ever before had been at such a ferocious depth without a diving helmet and lived to tell about it. When he left the submarine it was nearly dusk and he paused momentarily on the ascending line to marvel at the scene around him. The effect of the last rays of the sun as they filtered through the water made it seem as if he were suspended in the middle of an incredibly brilliant moonlit night. Below him the white sand bottom was spotted with sponges and clumps of gently waving grass while the S-4 stretched out in front of him like some great slumbering sea monster. From it now came a silent column of glistening air bubbles to scare off sharks. None were nosing about, however, and as he looked up all he could see were the spectral shapes of a half-dozen ships on the surface waiting for him to appear. They seemed so distant, but at the sight of them he finally shook free from his reverie and continued his ascent.

For Swede Momsen "well done" wires poured in from the White House on down. And the Navy added something extra— the Distinguished Service Medal. "Lieutenant Momsen," the citation read in part, "repeatedly and voluntarily risked his life in conducting experiments of a nature such that there was little or no information available as to their probable results. . . . It is through [his] initiative, courage and perseverance . . . that the development of the lung . . . reached a successful conclusion."

But more important for Momsen was an announcement from

the Secretary of the Navy that contracts had been let for seven thousand lungs.* Henceforth every new submarine would be equipped with escape hatches and locks; they were also to be installed as rapidly as possible in the seventy-five submarines already in service.

Now, a decade later, the *Squalus* was down.

Momsen, even though he had been given only the sketchiest report of what had happened to her, chose the three men allowed him on his first flight from Washington without hesitation. They would, he reasoned, backstop him in any emergency that might develop before the rescue chamber arrived.

One, in case a sudden descent had to be made to the *Squalus*, was a master diver, Chief Metalsmith James McDonald, co-holder of a record 500-foot descent in the pressure tank while testing the new helium and oxygen mixtures. The other two, Lieutenants O. D. Yarbrough and Albert Behnke, were both Navy doctors attached to Momsen's experimental diving unit; their presence would be crucial if the men in the *Squalus* were forced to brave forty freezing fathoms of the North Atlantic with the lung.

Halfway to Portsmouth, some two hours after their departure, Momsen was still preoccupied with dozens of unanswered questions about the condition of the *Squalus* when Behnke tapped him on the shoulder and shouted over the roar of the plane's motors, "I have a feeling we're going to do it!"

---

* The Navy also made the Momsen lung patents available to all nations. The British, however, preferred to wait for their own version developed by R. H. Davis. There has since been considerable confusion over which one came first. Even Captain Jacques-Yves Cousteau, the famous underwater explorer, gives the nod to Davis. But in the House of Commons on November 13, 1929, more than a year after Momsen's Potomac ascent and six months following adoption of his lung, First Lord of the Admiralty Alexander made the facts quite clear. In answer to a question regarding Royal Navy efforts to save submariners, Alexander said that tests had just been completed of the Davis Submerged Escape Apparatus, which "is similar in principle to the American lung."

Momsen's appreciative grin was short-lived. The chief pilot, Lieutenant Seymour Johnson, had come back with bad news about the weather. "It's closing in fast at Portsmouth," he said. "I'll do the best I can, but I'm not making any promises."

In Portsmouth the tug *Penacook* with Admiral Cole aboard nosed down the Piscataqua River at 1:30 P.M. that May 23rd. An ancient vessel, the best she could manage was about seven knots. Cole, however, was not especially troubled at the moment by her lack of speed. The important thing was that the *Sculpin* had finally discovered the whereabouts of the *Squalus* and was standing by her sister ship; little more could be done until the rescue fleet being assembled reached the scene.

Ten minutes later whatever comfort Cole had begun to allow himself disappeared when he was handed a radio message with chilling words from the *Sculpin:* "Cable on marker buoy parted. Am anchoring over *Squalus* position. Wait further instructions."

Nothing could have been more unexpected—or threatened more baleful consequences. The marker-buoy cable was, of course, a vital communications link between the *Squalus* and the surface. But beyond that it was the only available guide for a diver in attaching the second cable which the rescue chamber had to have to get to the sunken submarine. Without it days, even weeks, might be spent trying to find the *Squalus;* a diver working on his own in such depths could flounder blindly on the bottom practically next to her and never know it.

Perched in the *Penacook*'s wheelhouse, Cole was badly shaken. All that morning, immersed initially in his attempts to learn what had happened to the *Squalus* and then in launching a rescue operation, he had never entertained the possibility of ultimate failure. Now, for the first time, the ugly thought occurred to him.

The tension showed in the words he directed at the *Penacook*'s commander, Chief Boatswain David Ullman. "Goddammit," he snapped, "can't we do any better than this?" Ullman, who had never been on the receiving end of a flag officer's wrath before, somehow managed to coax a couple of extra knots out of her wheezing boiler, but it still took a frustrating hour before the black silhouette of the *Sculpin* could be seen riding sentinel on the horizon and the better part of another before the *Penacook* at last came alongside her.

Whether the cable would have parted if it had not been fastened to a deck cleat on the *Sculpin* was a question Cole let pass; his first concern was to relocate the *Squalus* at all costs. From the *Sculpin*'s Warren Wilkin he learned that as soon as the break was discovered, a second buoy had been anchored as close to the spot as possible. Then the *Sculpin* got a bearing with her supersonic gear on what was believed to be the *Squalus*. The fix, however, was only approximate and that far down, approximate just wasn't good enough.

Cole, once he had been briefed, was down to his last move until more help arrived. He instructed David Ullman on the *Penacook* to drop buoys a hundred yards north and south of the indicated position of the *Squalus* and to start dragging between them. "I don't have any time for speeches," Cole told Ullman. "You must find the *Squalus*."

Fifteen minutes later, both buoys in place, the *Penacook* began her lonely sweeps. As she did, a Coast Guard patrol plane lumbered in under the cloud blanket and started circling in lazy figure eights on watch for any members of the *Squalus* who might suddenly pop to the surface using Momsen lungs.

Just seeing this first tangible sign of the great rescue operation being mobilized lifted everyone's spirits. Cole himself had transferred to the *Sculpin* where messages piling into her radio room reported the progress of efforts elsewhere. The big seagoing tug

Wandank that Cole requested from the Boston Navy Yard had already quit her berth. Several Coast Guard cutters and patrol boats, which would ferry men and material from Portsmouth, were under way. Lieutenant Commander Momsen, Cole was advised, was expected to arrive by air from Washington early in the evening; his experimental diving unit would follow.

In New York the heavy cruiser *Brooklyn* with her medical facilities and thousands of extra feet of air hose on her decks slipped past the lower Manhattan skyline; she departed so hastily that nearly a third of her crew was left ashore. Behind her labored the tug *Sagamore* with nine salvage pontoons and a derrick lighter in tow.

The most cheering news of all came from New London. In an extraordinary response to the disaster, despite her almost complete lack of readiness that morning, the *Falcon*'s rescue chamber and her full complement of divers were back on board within an hour after final confirmation had been received that the *Squalus* was on the bottom. As she steamed down the Thames River, the first man Cole had turned to that morning, Captain Richard Edwards, the New London Commandant and Commander of Submarine Squadron Two which included the *Falcon*, prepared to depart for the scene on the destroyer *Semmes*. What bothered Edwards more than anything else now were the latest meteorological bulletins; a heavy fog was predicted for the southern New England coast that could raise hob with the *Falcon*'s arrival.

To the north, off the Isles of Shoals, Admiral Cole would worry about the weather later. At the moment all the divers and rescue chambers in the world were useless without some place to go. And as Cole watched on the bridge of the *Sculpin* his eyes never left the *Penacook* while she slowly maneuvered between the boundary buoys that he had ordered dropped before she started to grope along the ocean floor for the *Squalus*.

For everyone the *Penacook* was a familiar Portsmouth sight puttering about the harbor on routine chores. Now there was something wildly incongruous in seeing her cast in such a dramatic role. Technically Chief Boatswain Ullman could not be called her captain since she was not a commissioned vessel; his official designation was officer-in-charge. Because of her lowly status the poor *Penacook* could not even wear Navy gray. Instead she was painted a drab brown.

Standing next to Cole, Captain Halford Greenlee, with thoughts of his son-in-law uppermost in his mind, finally blurted out, "Do you think she can do it?"

"I don't know," Cole said, "but she's all we've got."

On the *Penacook* Ullman, acting as his own helmsman, had just completed his third fruitless pass over the supposed position of the *Squalus* when a deckhand tending the dragline came into the wheelhouse with word of what he had already begun to suspect. Her grapnel was too light to reach the bottom.

Ullman decided to try once more, reducing the *Penacook*'s speed so that she barely maintained steerageway, hoping that this might allow the grapnel to settle low enough in the water to be effective. When this didn't work, Ullman had no choice. He ordered the dragline taken in and reported back to Cole.

The tough little Admiral was not through yet. After an anxious huddle with Lieutenant Commander Wilkin, he gave instructions to replace the *Penacook*'s grappling irons with a spare anchor that the *Sculpin* carried. It at least proved heavy enough. Back and forth, dragging it now, the stubby tug toiled, the whitecaps whipping higher, the billowing overcast not much farther up than the *Squalus* was down.

The problem Ullman faced is easily duplicated. Just toss a fountain pen out of a third-story window, blindfold yourself and fish for the pen from the window with a piece of twine and a bent pin. Time after time the *Penacook*'s makeshift grapple caught hold of something and then slipped mockingly free. The Isles of Shoals were aptly named; scattered on the bottom along with the *Squalus* were scores of rotting hulks, some a century or more old.

The lowering clouds had forced the patrol plane to abandon its watch overhead and a light rain was falling when the tug *Wandank* hove to next to the *Sculpin* at 5:20 P.M. Cole immediately put her powerful underwater oscillator to work in an attempt to call the *Squalus*. Back through the ocean depths came the feeble sound of hammer taps. A few minutes later, just as the *Penacook* was starting another swing, a rocket from the *Squalus* burst above the surface. It was at best a general guide. Even more maddening for Ullman, it exploded over an area he had already covered twice.

At 5:45 the civilian tug *Chandler* arrived with a doctor, three pharmacist's mates and fifty blankets from the Portsmouth Naval Hospital. Two Coast Guard cutters were also on the scene.

On the *Penacook* Ullman barely noticed the new arrivals. His warrant as a chief boatswain testified to his seamanship and he needed every bit of savvy he possessed to handle his unwieldy charge, with her trailing anchor, in the steadily rising sea. A slightly built man, he had clung tenaciously to the wheel for more than four hours, raising a hand from it only to gulp down cups of coffee, as he patiently probed the bottom. His brow was permanently furrowed from the vicious migraine headaches he periodically suffered. The possibility that he might have one now was of some concern to Admiral Cole, but Ullman was gripped by a zeal that left no room for headaches. He was certain he would locate the *Squalus* and he was determined to keep up the hunt all night if necessary.

Then at 7:30, in the gathering darkness, the *Penacook* again snagged something almost on a direct line between the buoys marking the search area; this time the big iron hook held.

5

No one item of news dominated the headlines on the morning of May 23, 1939. In Berlin, with Hitler looking on, Germany and Italy signed a ten-year pact to "remake" Europe, but this simply confirmed what everybody had been expecting. In Tokyo the Japanese announced that they had successfully wound up another week's wholesale carnage in China. In Washington President Roosevelt denounced critics of the New Deal who said it was hurting small business. In Quebec the visiting British monarchs, King George VI and Queen Elizabeth, met the Dionne quints for the first time. In London Ambassador Joseph P. Kennedy told a group of English tailors that they would never crack the American market if they kept making trouser waistlines too high and shirttails too long.

In New York City the Most Reverend Francis J. Spellman was formally installed as Archbishop in ceremonies at Saint Patrick's Cathedral. Bloomingdale's Department Store was advertising the hours when its customers could see a new gadget called television and United Airlines ballyhooed its new nonstop flight to Chicago that took only four hours and thirty-five minutes.

In baseball a young center fielder for the New York Yankees named Joe DiMaggio was headed for his first batting championship. Rudy Vallee was appearing at the Astor Roof on Times Square and the movie *Wuthering Heights* with the new English actor Laurence Olivier was in its sixth smash week at the Roxy. In the theatre Tallulah Bankhead was starring in *The Little Foxes* and Katharine Hepburn in *The Philadelphia Story*. A novel destined to become an American classic, Nathanael West's *The Day of the Locust,* was reviewed in the *New York Times,* where it was dismissed as "vulgar" and "cheap."

The story that seemed likely to attract the most national attention in the afternoon was an industry-wide automobile strike. Some 65,000 workers had already left their jobs. Then every editor in the country forgot about the walkout. The first stark bulletin flashed over the Associated Press wire just after 2 P.M. in time to catch late editions of evening newspapers in the East: "SUBMARINE SQUALUS DOWN OFF NEW ENGLAND COAST WITH SIXTY-TWO MEN ON BOARD."

(The miscount in the number of men the *Squalus* carried, sixty-two instead of fifty-nine, was corrected later in the day by Admiral Cole's aide, Lieutenant Commander Curley, who had remained in Portsmouth to coordinate communications. Curley's initial announcement to a handful of local stringers was based on the *Squalus* roster for the previous Friday. It included two civilian technicians who had finished their work earlier than expected because of the submarine's nearly flawless trial runs. The third man presumed on board at first, Machinist's Mate First Class Donald Savage, was in the Portsmouth Naval Hospital recovering from the beaning he had suffered on Sunday playing softball.)

Like many reporters, pioneer CBS News correspondent Bob

Trout thought he was getting to Portsmouth the quickest possible way—by air. Trout was in a Manhattan studio rehearsing a featured spot he had on the Hal Kemp "Time to Shine Show." Right in the middle of it he was called by the network's Director of Special Events and ordered to Newark Airport where he was to hop on an amphibian CBS had chartered. Trout dashed out of the studio while the program's outraged advertising agency man chased after him shouting, "You can't do this to me!"

There was considerable haze as Trout took off, but he could clearly see the Trylon and Perisphere of the New York World's Fair off to his right as the plane headed for Long Island Sound. Along the Connecticut shore, however, his pilot had to fly at five hundred feet to get under the heavy cloud cover. Then, just as they were passing over the Yale Bowl in New Haven, fog completely enveloped them. The pilot, Trout recalls, "dipped, wheeled and dived, banked out over the water and then back inland almost to Hartford" before he finally gave up and grounded Trout in New London.

Outside Captain Greenlee's red-brick residence on the crest of a small hill some fifty yards behind the administration building at the Portsmouth Navy Yard, two Marines had taken up guard duty. By the time Greenlee's son Bob brought his sister Betty and Mrs. Naquin there in response to his father's telephone call, Greenlee himself had rushed home to speak to them briefly before boarding the *Penacook* with Admiral Cole. His daughter-in-law Jacqueline remembers him as white-faced but calm.

"We're still not sure what went wrong," he said. "The *Squalus* is in trouble and probably on the bottom. But there's every reason to believe that Pat and Oliver are all right. Just a few minutes ago the *Sculpin* reported sighting a smoke bomb and under the circumstances that's the best news we could have."

After he left, Bob and Jacqueline Greenlee went off to round up the other wives of the *Squalus* officers who were supposed to attend the bridge luncheon for their *Sculpin* counterparts. Inside the house Betty Patterson quietly embraced her mother and placed a call to her husband's parents in Enid, Oklahoma.

As it was being put through, Frances Naquin stared blankly out of a window. All she could think of now was driving down to the mouth of the Piscataqua with her two children the previous evening to visit the overnight anchorage of the *Squalus* and not being able to wave to her husband because of the rain. A minor disappointment at the time, it suddenly seemed so terribly important and she could not help wondering if it had been a sinister portent of what was to come. Then she silently upbraided herself for such thoughts. As the wife of the commanding officer of the *Squalus* she had a special responsibility to meet—for him as well as herself.

Other calls were going out from the yard now. About a third of the *Squalus* crewmen had installed their wives and families in apartments or rented bungalows behind the fine old colonial homes that dotted Portsmouth and its sister city of Kittery, Maine, across the Piscataqua. But rumors of what had happened spread quickly through the close-knit Navy community, and before official word reached many of them, grim-faced women were streaming over the bridge that connected the yard proper with Kittery.

Lieutenant Commander Curley did his best to reassure them as they crowded into the administration building. His task, delicate enough as it was, would have been infinitely more difficult had not a gap in communications developed during those first hectic hours between Portsmouth and the scene of the disaster. In the brief conversation the *Sculpin* held with the *Squalus* before the marker-buoy cable snapped, there had been no specific mention of any casualties; so when nothing more was heard on the subject through the afternoon, Portsmouth simply presumed that all hands on the sunken submarine were alive.

This misconception continued well into the night of May 23rd, even after the *Sculpin* had ascertained that only thirty-three members of the trapped crew could be accounted for. The message back to Portsmouth that the men in the forward compartments of the *Squalus* were in "satisfactory condition" neglected to note their number.

Most of the women, relieved of their greatest fear at least temporarily and ready to grasp at any straw, took their cue from Mrs. Lawrence Gainor, wife of the Chief Electrician's Mate who had disconnected the forward battery switches as the *Squalus* plunged to the bottom. In tones as laconic as her husband might have used, she said, "He's been in scrapes before. He'll be all right."

Frances Naquin echoed this optimistic line later in the day. In a statement Curley released to the press, she cited the massive rescue efforts the Navy was making and voiced her confidence that "the whole thing will be over tomorrow."

For some, however, a sickening question remained. Could the men, even if they still survived, escape entombment at a depth no submariner had ever defied before? And nowhere did it show more plainly than in the anguished face of Mrs. John Chestnutt, whose husband had been the newest chief on board the *Squalus*. All that afternoon and into the night she walked ceaselessly about the base, clutching her young son by the hand, striding from the administration building up to the Greenlee residence, back down to the waterfront and across the bridge into Kittery, stopping there only to retrace her route. Not once in her tormented journey was the boy seen to complain.

For Mrs. Donald Smith, wife of the General Motors representative on board the *Squalus* to check out the engines, there was the special hell of what might have been. The young diesel expert earlier in the year had been in the submarine *Permit* when she briefly went aground underwater while on a trial run off Halifax, Nova Scotia. The experience had been an unnerving one and with a nine-month-old baby, their first, to think about now, the Smiths did considerable soul-searching on whether this was the kind of work he ought to be in. But finally they decided that such fears were silly and Smith went ahead and bought a home in Portsmouth where he would be GM's regular man at the Navy yard.

The release of the names of the trapped crewmen and their home towns sent reporters around the country ferreting out relatives. In Boston the mother of Quartermaster First Class Francis Murphy, with all the dark distrust she had harbored about submarines, provided quite a story. "My boy," she declared, "said the *Squalus* was stuck for more than an hour while on a week's cruise that ended last Friday." According to Mrs. Murphy, her son told her that if the *Squalus* had been fifty feet lower "we would have been cooked," and on a visit over the weekend he had asked her to pray for him. "My boy," she concluded, "knew something was going to happen!"

Mrs. Murphy's comments were duly noted and clipped by Navy Intelligence. At the time rescue ships were still hurrying to the scene, another operation had already been launched—which in the months ahead would painstakingly seek to discover how and why the last word in American submarine design lay crippled now on the ocean floor.

In New York Seaman William Boulton's wife, Rita, first heard the news on the radio. She had gone down from Portsmouth on Sunday night to help her sister care for their ailing mother. At a party before she left Portsmouth, she recalled, one of the crew with a little too much beer in him kept roaring that nothing could ever sink the *Squalus,* until somebody finally shut him up. But what the twenty-year-old Mrs. Boulton, married only a few months, remembered most were her husband's parting words. "Kiss me again," he had said, "just for luck."

In Washington Mrs. Richard Isaacs, mother of the cook on duty as the morning dive began, was at a neighbor's house when she also heard over the radio what had happened. "Oh, those poor fellows!" she exclaimed. Beyond that, however, she was not unduly alarmed. Mrs. Isaacs was sure that the name of her son's submarine was the *Sculpin*. But when she returned home, touched by the thought that he could just as easily as not have been among the missing sailors, she took out a Mother's Day card he had sent her. To her horror, she saw that the return address on the envelope was "c/o U.S.S. *Squalus.*"

A few blocks away Torpedoman Second Class Alfred Priester's wife sat cradling their two-year-old son in her arms. "I've never experienced anything like this before," she said. "I know there's nothing I can do except pray to God that Al is safe." Then Mrs. Priester spoke haltingly about her plan to spend some time in Portsmouth with her husband the following month. She had to stop constantly to correct herself; she kept talking about it in the past tense.

All these women, wherever they were, at least had somebody they could turn to for comfort. But for the Rumanian-born wife of Torpedoman First Class Robert Gibbs, there was no one. Mrs. Gibbs had already left the home of her husband's parents in Lexington, South Carolina, when the first radio reports were broadcast. The family immediately contacted an uncle of Gibbs, F. O. Barrett, who worked in Washington at the Government Printing Office. Barrett got down to Union Station in time to intercept the train and rushed through it paging her. Finally he found Mrs. Gibbs, a slender, sad-eyed woman with her hair drawn back tightly in a bun, seated in one of the rear coaches. As Barrett tried to identify himself and explain why he was there, he realized that her English was not up to it. In desperation he pointed to a newspaper headline about the *Squalus*. Just then the train started moving again and Barrett, not knowing what else he could do, jumped off. Mrs. Gibbs would ride alone all the way to Portsmouth, still not sure what was wrong, aware only that something terrible had befallen her husband.

Inside the *Squalus* the worst part was the damp, gnawing cold. And the waiting. It was dark in the two crowded compartments—eighteen men in the control room; fifteen more in the forward torpedo room—except for the dim glow of the hand lanterns.

In the control room valves wheezed and hissed sporadically under the backed-up water pressure. Beneath soggy blankets the men huddled together on mattresses or directly on the linoleum deck; others sat with their backs against the bulkheads, their knees drawn up under their chins. Many of them were still wet from the first onrush of the sea. Nobody talked. They moved as little as possible. Occasionally there was a cough, a sudden sneeze or the incoherent moan of a man drugged into half sleep by the fouled air. Near each of them was a Momsen lung in case some new emergency forced a quick exit from the ship or to don as masks if chlorine gas started seeping in from the forward battery.

When his conversation with Wilkin on the *Sculpin* ended so abruptly, Naquin continued to maintain a telephone watch, hopeful that whatever had caused the break in the connection would be corrected, never dreaming at first that the cable itself might have separated.

By two o'clock that afternoon the cold inside the *Squalus* had increased noticeably and the last of the oilskin raincoats in the control-room locker were handed out. Something else could no

longer be ignored. As the men exhaled, they filled the compartment with carbon dioxide; a can of special absorbent was opened
and about a quarter of it was sprinkled on the deck.

Along with the CO_2 absorbent, Naquin also had a supply of
pure oxygen stored in flasks to guard against suffocation. But he
was determined to husband it as long as he could. He had no idea
how long it would take to get down to them and the silence on the
surface was disturbing him more every minute. Although he had a
carbon dioxide analysis kit, he decided against drawing more
attention than necessary to the problem by using it. Instead, he
gauged the quality of the air by the amount of nausea and difficulty
in breathing among the men. He purposely kept the air slightly on
the toxic side. It made the men drowsy; they were less apt to move
around and the time seemed to go faster.

When the *Penacook* arrived on the scene, the sound of her
propellers could be clearly heard inside the *Squalus*. The men were
immensely heartened by the presence of still another ship. But as
the little tug unaccountably began passing back and forth overhead, it did not take long for them to conclude that direct contact
with the *Squalus* had somehow been lost and that the *Penacook*
was now grappling for her. "Anyway," Electrician's Mate First
Class Judson Bland muttered, "they know we're down here somewhere."

This stoicism under pressure, displayed by all his men, greatly
affected Naquin. Not once had there been a sign of fear, a
complaint about the cold, a wail of impatience or despair. Instinctively they shared their blankets in the packed floor space or lay in
each other's arms to try to keep warm. It suddenly occurred to
Naquin that he was witnessing a phenomenon usually associated
with hackneyed Sunday sermons—"brotherly love."

At 4:30 P.M. Naquin made another inspection tour to the
forward torpedo room. As he passed through the forward battery,
he ruefully noted how much warmer it was than either of the two

compartments his men occupied. But Naquin could already detect the first faint whiffs of chlorine gas forming in there.

When he got to the forward torpedo room, he immediately conferred with Nichols. In his initial instructions to the young officer, Naquin had told him to relay over the marker-buoy phone his suspicion that the main engine air-induction valve was the cause of all their trouble. He also told Nichols to recommend that divers be sent down to close the valve and attach hoses to pump out the flooded compartments. But in the uncertain moments following the loss of voice communication with the *Sculpin*, Naquin forgot to find out if Nichols had time enough to pass on the message before he took the phone himself. Now, to his satisfaction, he learned that his directions had been carried out to the letter; after thinking about it all afternoon it seemed to him a much better plan than relying on the rescue chamber.

At 4:45 additional CO_2 absorbent was spread in both compartments. For the first time oxygen flasks were bled to improve the air. Then, as the *Squalus* went into her ninth hour on the bottom, a supper of canned beans, tomatoes and pineapple was ladled out. Once more pineapple was the only item that perked up any real interest among the men.

A few minutes later the pulsing beat of powerful new screws reached the *Squalus*. At precisely 5:21, according to Francis Murphy's log, the shrill ping of an oscillator identified the new arrival as the *Wandank* and requested acknowledgment. The reply in Morse code fell to Radioman First Class Arthur Booth and Signalman Second Class Warren Smith. Setting themselves inside the conning tower, they peeled back part of its cork lining and took turns pounding against the steel skin of the *Squalus* with small sledge hammers, one stroke for a dot and two for a dash. Inside the submarine the sound of the hammer blows was deafening. But could they be picked up on the surface?

A hush so strained you could almost physically feel it spread through the *Squalus*. Five minutes passed. Then ten more. After twenty minutes Naquin said, "Cravens, send up a rocket." The veteran Gunner's Mate, who had had so much trouble opening his first canister of rockets for the morning firings, was ready. At 5:43 it went up.

Still there was nothing. Suddenly the silence in the control room was broken by a half-stifled cry. Ever since supper Seaman Second Class Robert Washburn had been trying to fight off an attack of chills. The young sailor, on board his first submarine, had started the day with a bad cold. Then in escaping from the after battery he had been thoroughly soaked. Now he could no longer hold out; his teeth began to chatter uncontrollably and his body was racked by violent shivering.

Naquin was at his side at once. He whipped off his foul-weather jacket and put it around Washburn's shoulders. Pharmacist's Mate First Class Raymond O'Hara was right behind Naquin. He placed his blanket over the young seaman, got a slicker from another man and then held Washburn tightly to him. That was all O'Hara could do except whisper, "Take it easy, kid, you'll be okay."

At 6:04 P.M. the *Wandank*'s oscillator started up again. But the message failed to resolve the question of whether the hammer taps were getting to the surface. "Can you hear us?" the *Wandank* asked.

In the conning tower Warren Smith pounded back, "Yes."

Fifteen minutes dragged by without anything further from the *Wandank*, and Naquin, concerned that there had been no reaction to his plan for raising the *Squalus*, decided to try a message of his own. Smith and Booth, alternating on each word, beat it out: "Will you apply salvage air to compartments abaft control room? We have air for ballast tanks."

But the *Wandank*'s next set of signals left Naquin as nonplused as ever. They bore no relation to his query and he could only assume that the *Squalus* was just too far down for hammering on the hull to be effective. "How many officers and crew in unflooded compartments?" the *Wandank* now wanted to know. "Are you taking water in those compartments?"

With little hope that it would do much good, Naquin dictated a terse reply: "Thirty-three; negative." What made the whole thing all the more infuriating was the beautiful clarity of the *Wandank*'s signals. Naquin felt like a man in a nightmare standing on a busy street corner while throngs of people oblivious to his shouts passed him by.

Then, as the clang of the hammers died away in the vastness of the North Atlantic, the news came that two-way communications, however tenuous, had been established at last. "We can hear your hammering," the *Wandank* reported, "but very weak. Send each word three times." The ragged cheer inside the submarine quickly subsided as the *Wandank* continued signaling: "What degree list?"

Once more Warren Smith and Arthur Booth went to work. They had taken incredible punishment. The cold in the conning tower was far worse than either the forward torpedo room or the control room and the air was just as bad. But, gasping for breath and choking down waves of nausea, they had never let up for a moment as they hammered out a steady tattoo of dots and dashes. Now, their efforts finally rewarded, they banged away with renewed fury.

Naquin kept his answer as brief as he could: "No list but eleven degree angle up by bow." Even so, it took Smith and Booth half an hour to send it. As Smith completed the last word for the third time, he found himself, despite the frigid temperature, bathed in a clammy sweat. Then he threw up.

Naquin called both men back into the control room. The job would be continued by Radioman Second Class Charles Powell and Signalman Third Class Theodore Jacobs in the forward torpedo room. As Smith and Booth staggered down from the conning tower, Naquin was about to order those closest to them to share their blankets. But before he could say anything it was already being done.

Five minutes later, at 7:30, Naquin became vaguely aware that there was a change in their situation. It took him a minute more to put his finger on it. The dull throb of the *Penacook*'s propellers had suddenly ceased. He discounted the idea that the weather was to blame; surely if it had become a problem the *Wandank* would have mentioned it. There was only one other possibility he could think of. The tug had hooked the *Squalus*—or thought she had.

Naquin anxiously awaited some confirmation of this. But when none was forthcoming by eight o'clock, he instructed Powell and Jacobs to tap out, "Have you located us?" There was no answer. At 8:30 Naquin tried again, "What are plans on surface?"

To his dismay, however, all he got was another query, this one requesting a description of current conditions on board the *Squalus*. Just four words long and directed as much to his own men as to the surface, Naquin's reply—"Conditions satisfactory but cold"—would electrify millions of morning newspaper readers still under the mistaken impression that the entire crew had thus far been spared.

Then at 9:10 the *Wandank*'s oscillator unexpectedly relayed what Naquin had been striving to find out ever since the *Penacook* stopped passing back and forth overhead: "Believe have grapnel attached your ship."

Naquin fervently hoped so. But there was a nasty little fact that he could not ignore. Nothing had been heard or felt inside the *Squalus* which gave the slightest indication that a grappling iron had taken hold of her.

On the bridge of the *Falcon* a hundred and fifty miles to the south, Lieutenant George Sharp cursed his luck. Once clear of the

Thames River and in Long Island Sound, Sharp planned to save time by cutting inside Fishers Island, the millionaire retreat southeast of the mouth of the Thames. But almost immediately he ran into a thick fog bank that made this too treacherous to chance and Sharp had to go the long way around.

The *Falcon* was one of a number of vessels built in 1917 to sweep the seas of German mines. Five of these "bird boats," as they were called, were later converted into rescue and salvage ships and assigned to key submarine commands around the world—the *Falcon* at New London, the *Mallard* at Coco Solo in the Canal Zone, the *Ortolan* at San Diego, the *Widgeon* at Pearl Harbor and the *Pigeon* at Cavite in the Philippines.

Along with a rescue chamber, each carried a high- and low-pressure air system for diving and salvage work, a recompression chamber and all the complex gear for divers themselves. But they also represented the one complete defeat Swede Momsen had suffered in his efforts to bring submarine rescue to optimum efficiency.

His objections to them were multiple. Their maximum speed, around twelve knots, was hardly adequate when time might be the decisive factor in an underwater disaster. Only 188 feet long with a thirty-seven foot beam, their limited deck and storage space made the handling of literally miles of air hoses, manila lines, steel cables and chains a nightmare. And, most prophetic in the case of the *Squalus,* their lightweight displacement of 1,600 tons would leave them at the mercy of anything less than ideal surface conditions during a rescue operation.

But while Momsen failed to get ships specifically tailored for the job, he did manage to engineer one policy change. Until 1929 bird-boat skippers had been selected with little regard for their previous experience. Since then, however, they were required to have both submarine and diving backgrounds. In a Navy whose whole theoretical thrust put a premium on all-round ability over specialization for line officers, Momsen gently touched on the pyschological importance of the move. "In this instance," he argued, "it is essential that there be a commanding officer who speaks the particular language of the diver and who thoroughly understands submarine rescue and escape problems."

Sharp himself had just come off submarine duty to captain the *Falcon* and it didn't tax his imagination much to visualize what it must be like inside the *Squalus*. Now he took the weather that had closed in around him as a personal affront. The *Falcon*, by any standard, was a ship of destiny. Not only had she been on hand for almost all of Momsen's experiments with the lung and bell, but as she nosed through the fog toward the stricken *Squalus*, it seemed as if she were on a ghostly course into her own past. A few miles to the starboard were the waters that had closed over the *S-51* and later would come Massachusetts Bay where the *S-4* met her awful end. Each time she stood by to no avail. This third time, however, there was a difference—the rescue chamber on her fantail. Up ahead the Cape Cod Canal had been alerted to keep free of all traffic for the *Falcon*'s passage. But it would be early morning at best before she could reach the *Squalus*.

In the isolation of the Greenlee home the wives of the *Squalus* officers sat tensely waiting throughout the afternoon and evening. Jacqueline Greenlee's task was to screen telephone calls from anxious friends and to take periodic reports from Lieutenant Commander Curley. Around 5 P.M. she was amazed to find herself connected on an overseas line with a London newspaper. "With the London call," she says, "we suddenly woke up to the fact that the whole world was watching and waiting with us."

In New London a frustrated Bob Trout finally caught a night express which would get him to Dover, New Hampshire, about twenty miles up the Piscataqua from Portsmouth. The station-master had assured Trout that while his own quota of sleeping compartments happened to be sold out, he would have no trouble obtaining space once he was on board. But Trout was lucky to land the last available upper berth. The train was jammed with re-porters, photographers, newscasters, radio technicians and newsreel cameramen, all in the same fix he was in. "There we were," Trout recalls, "supposedly covering a great disaster and we probably knew less about what was going on than anyone else."

Still, within three hours after the first flash, a vanguard of the newsmen swarming toward Portsmouth had arrived by car from nearby Boston and was already filing copy out of a pressroom hastily set up in the administration building.

As the evening wore on, speculation among the reporters there began to center increasingly on the flooded after sections of the *Squalus*. Curley continued to insist—the truth as he knew it—that there was no indication that any of the trapped crewmen were dead. But under persistent questioning, Curley acknowledged that he could not swear that every last man on board the submarine had made it safely into watertight compartments.

At midnight four Boston newsmen determined to settle the matter. Despite the weather, they hired a Kittery lobsterman to take them to the disaster scene. It was a trip none of them would ever forget. Within minutes after leaving the Piscataqua, as their open boat careened crazily in a six-foot chop, they were drenched and hideously seasick. It took three hours to complete the fifteen-mile trip, and when they finally drew as close as they dared to what turned out to be the *Wandank,* Harry Crockett of the Associated Press grabbed a megaphone and shouted to a shadowy figure on deck, "How many are dead down below?"

Back came the call that twenty-six of the crew had been caught in the after compartments and were believed lost. If anything, the return trip was worse, the seas running so high that Crockett was suddenly sent sprawling, his right hand slashed to the bone by a big lobsterman's hook. The reporters tottered ashore at the Navy yard just after daybreak, Crockett bleeding so badly that he looked as if he were wearing a "bright red glove." But he refused any treatment until he finished telephoning the story to his home office.

Only then did the *Squalus* women learn that some of their men would never come back. What remained for them now was the grisly question—which ones?

6

NORTH OF BOSTON, PILOT SEYMOUR JOHSON HAD MOMSEN, Drs. Behnke and Yarbrough and diver McDonald exchange their parachutes for life jackets. The ceiling had lifted barely enough for him to risk a landing in the Piscataqua. Swede Momsen didn't envy him one bit. Not even submarines with their powerful diesels attempted the river except at slack water. And now, with night fast approaching, there were all those spar buoys, can buoys and beacons that dotted its twisting course to think about. But at 7:30, just as the *Penacook* had hopefully hooked the *Squalus,* Johnson splashed down beautifully.

"Say, that was all right," Momsen told him.

For once he was topped. "Well, sir," Johnson replied with a straight face, "I didn't have much choice, did I?"

At the Portsmouth Navy Yard Momsen, with news-camera flashbulbs popping off around him, boarded a Coast Guard cutter for the last leg of the trip. The rain that had been falling intermittently since late afternoon had started again and he shivered in the New England chill. He realized suddenly that all the clothes he had with him were his light cotton suit and the now-bedraggled panama hat he had sported to work that morning. Somebody on the cutter gave him a foul-weather coat. It was, he thought, a hell of an outfit to be wearing at a time like this.

As always, there was nothing impersonal about what he was getting into this fateful May 23rd. Momsen knew most of the officers and some of the men on the *Squalus*. He also knew Harold Preble especially well; as a matter of fact he had been carrying on a year-long dispute by mail with Preble over the accuracy of several stop watches he had requisitioned at Portsmouth during diving experiments the previous June.

Gradually a weird glow appeared through the misty rain ahead of him. The scene grew even spookier as the cutter closed in on it. Riding at anchor in a rough circle some three hundred yards across were the *Sculpin* and the tugs *Wandank*, *Penacook* and *Chandler*, every searchlight they had flooding the area in and around a wooden grating to which the *Penacook* had tied her dragline. Around this perimeter two Coast Guard patrol boats, the *158* and *409*, slowly churned, their lights playing back and forth over the black, white-tipped waves, on guard for any of the *Squalus* crew surfacing without warning with the lung.

Momsen transferred to the *Sculpin* at 10:45 P.M. In the wardroom he was warmly greeted by Admiral Cole. "Swede," he said, "I want you take charge of all diving operations." To make it official, he sent a dispatch to all hands concerned. Then, for the first time, Momsen learned that the marker-buoy cable had parted. "We think we've located her," Cole said, "but we can't be positive."

Continuing his briefing, Cole told Momsen that contact of sorts was being maintained via hammer taps from the submarine. Subsequent to Naquin's dramatic report that conditions below

were satisfactory but cold and that thirty-three men were known to
be alive in the forward torpedo and control rooms, it had been
established that for the time being there were ample emergency
rations, drinking water and CO_2 absorbent and that the pressure
in the compartments still free of water was equal to a depth of
twenty-seven feet, almost double atmospheric pressure on the
surface.

"Is there anything else we ought to know?" Cole asked
Momsen.

"No, sir," he answered at once. "I think it would be a pretty
good idea if we kept any more queries to an absolute minimum.
Right now the best thing for them all is to stay quiet and conserve
every bit of energy they can. Hammering on the hull is just going
to tire them out."

"I agree," Cole said. "Nevertheless I want to send some message down to the men to let them know you're here. It will boost
their morale tremendously."

"That's very kind of you," Momsen replied. "In that case you
might tell them I said twenty-seven feet of pressure won't cause
any problems."

Cole then brought up Naquin's plan of pumping out the flooded
after sections of the *Squalus*. It had sounded so appealing that it
had been released to the press at Portsmouth as a rescue method
under prime consideration. But that was precisely the trouble—it
only *sounded* simple.

As the latest addition to Cole's rescue team—although he had in
effect just been given direct responsibility for getting the trapped
crew out—Momsen demurred as diplomatically as he could. While
an open main induction valve headed everybody's suspect list, it
was by no means a sure bet at this point. More important, linking
up the necessary salvage lines was a good deal easier to talk about
than do. Momsen was a qualified deep-sea diver himself and he

knew from experience exactly how a man's mental processes, supported by oxygen alone, would be reduced to an almost child-like state working in the fearful pressure of the ocean at a depth of 243 feet.

If the new helium mixtures were immediately available, which they were not, it would still remain a job of stupendous complexity. But even granting the remote possibility of initial success, there was no assurance that all the flooded compartments could be cleared, that sufficient air under pressure could be pumped in that far down, that the *Squalus* could then be quickly raised.

"Admiral," Momsen told Cole, "that's always been the problem. We never seem to have submarine disasters made to order in convenient locations. Those men are either going to come up themselves or we'll have to go down after them."

Momsen was somewhat critical on another count. But there was nothing he could do about it now, so he kept silent. Once the *Sculpin* had arrived on the scene, he would not have shared in the general reluctance to use the lung. His faith in it was based on something more than sentiment. Following its adoption by the Navy, Momsen had begun work on plans for two ingenious 138-foot-high lung-training tanks, at New London and Pearl Harbor, the tank proper in each instance a hundred feet deep with intermediate locks fifty and eighteen feet from the top. Nearly a thousand men had mastered his artifical lung in them when suddenly two deaths were reported in rapid succession, both in eighteen feet of water.

For Momsen it had been a bad moment. It was incredible to think that a person could kill himself coming up at a depth a swimmer of ordinary ability could reach without harm. He had always been worried about some hidden danger during the lung's early development. "Have I," Momsen wrote with bitter reproach in his diary, "been lulled into a false sense of security by the success of my own personal experiments?"

Since the Navy was publicly committed to the new device, the matter was kept under wraps while the Bureau of Medicine and Surgery began an urgent study of the fatal accidents in collaboration with Harvard University's School of Public Health. But once again the lung itself was not at fault; instead, another fledging step was achieved in unlocking the mysterious forces man faced in the sea. The two men had died simply because they had held their breath.

The answer—so routine today, so unknown then—was that a swimmer diving from the surface starts with a lungful of air that contracts in the increased water pressure he encounters. But someone only eighteen feet down who fills his lungs with air or oxygen takes in over half as much as he would on the surface even though it occupies the same amount of space. If he holds his breath, it immediately begins to expand as he rises. Specialists at Harvard discovered that just two pounds of excess pressure against human lungs were enough to drive deadly air bubbles into the bloodstream and thence to the brain. At eighteen feet this pressure would mount to more than eight pounds. After he got the news, Momsen recalled the stories he had heard about men lost at sea in great depths "blowing up" when their bodies came to the surface; maybe, he reflected, they were not fables after all.

From then on, however, everything went smoothly. And, like every submariner, each *Squalus* crewman had to qualify with the lung before being accepted for underseas duty. Not even the frigid waters in which she plunged, of such concern to Cole and Naquin, would have swayed Momsen had he arrived sooner. After he had completed his dramatic trials with the lung off Key West, his old nemesis, the Bureau of Construction and Repair, noted that "we might be remiss" if he was not prepared to say how his new device would fare in chillier climates. "It was," he once remarked, "the most subtle directive I ever received during my naval career."

So the following January found Momsen on the *Falcon* as she towed the *S-4* to a point eighty feet deep off Block Island. The day was fiercely cold, the sky sullenly overcast, the ocean temperature an inhospitable thirty-three degrees. To top off the whole thing, just as he and his favorite diving partner, Edward Kalinoski, boarded the *S-4* for the trip down, it started snowing. As a test of endurance he could not have asked for better—or worse— conditions.

Dressed only in bathing suits, the two men waited until the icy water rose high enough to balance the pressure so they could swing open the hatch of their escape lock. Momsen went first, Kalinoski right behind, holding his foot for company. The only anxious time they had was when they reached the surface; it was snowing so hard that the *Falcon* was nowhere to be seen. But a small boat quickly moved in to pick them up, and once they were back on the *Falcon,* the same Dr. Yarbrough whom Momsen had brought with him on the flight to Portsmouth provided a special treat—a healthy jolt of grain alcohol in a mug of black coffee. It also made something of a legendary character out of Momsen. Though the service was sternly teetotaling at sea and prohibition was still the law of the land, a memo from him extolling the virtues of what he dubbed "Coffee Royal" resulted in an official change in the Navy's *Supply Manual* which allowed an issue of grain alcohol to all divers operating in cold water. "No man," one grateful beneficiary wrote him, "ever struck a greater blow for liberty!"

But now—the trapped *Squalus* crewmen already on the bottom for some fifteen hours, their strength inevitably sapped by the cold, the foul air, the intangible tensions of their plight—he agreed that they should fall back on the lung only as a last resort. So they would wait for the *Falcon*—and the rescue chamber.

That it was available at all was entirely Swede Momsen's doing. Despite his preoccupation with the lung, he had never abandoned his original concept of a diving bell. The chance to revive it came on the heels of the lung's first spectacular demonstration in the Potomac. Summoned to explain its workings before a special Presidential board on submarine safety belatedly set up following the loss of the *S-4*, Momsen finished his briefing and promptly launched into a pitch for the bell as well.

When a startled member of the civilian-dominated board demanded to know why the proposal had not previously been submitted to the Navy, there was an awkward pause before Momsen replied, "It was."

Given a green light at once, Momsen continued to test the lung while simultaneously starting with the bell. He remembered the experimental tank for carrying a seaplane on his old command, the *S-1*. The project had never really come to much and the tank as it happened was then being removed from the submarine. Cut in half, Momsen figured, it would make a perfect pilot model for what he had in mind.

The tank was at his request shipped to the Brooklyn Navy Yard where a bright young officer in the Construction Corps, Lieutenant Morgan Watt, began to transform his rough plans into detailed drawings. But there was more to it than that. With nothing more to rely on than their own imaginations, they always had hanging over their heads the awesome challenge of trying to anticipate all the uncharted perils of an actual rescue, where even the slightest factor overlooked now meant death later.

One of the bell's drawbacks as initially conceived by Momsen was getting it rapidly and precisely in place over a submarine hatch. His solution now was to have it do the work. A diver would be sent down to attach two cables to the hatch. The cables in turn led up to reels inside the bell, so that when the bell was lowered into the water with just enough ballast to keep it lightly afloat, it would wind itself directly down to the hatch. As many trips as necessary could be made to get the men out and up.

The idea of using a diver first led to the realization of still another lethal danger. A diver would be necessary in any event. A piece of debris, a loose line lying over the hatch would absolutely preclude the watertight seal that was so essential.

More refinements were added along the way as Momsen, busy preparing for his lung escapes off Key West, commuted back and forth from Florida. A hatch was put in the bell's top to make it easier for its operator to enter and rescued submariners to exit. Since partial or complete immersion of the motors running the reels could be expected, they would be powered by compressed air instead of electricity. To help solve the delicate problem of maintaining positive buoyancy—so that the bell would always float free of water by keeping the air pressure inside it equal to the sea pressure below—a green stripe was painted near its bottom edge; if the sea stayed below the stripe the bell would have positive buoyancy, but if it rose above the stripe negative buoyancy resulted and the bell would sink.

The finished product looked like a huge inverted tumbler, five feet in diameter and seven feet high. Before Momsen could arrive, however, Watt was so excited that he decided on a test of his own in a flooded dry dock at the yard. He discovered to his chagrin just how important the guide cables to the hatch were going to be. Without them it was next to impossible to control the bell. First he vented the air in it out. This, of course, made the bell heavier and it started to drop. But after Watt opened the compressed-air hose to stabilize his position, it didn't come in fast enough. Then when he hastily built up the pressure, the bell shot to the surface, promptly tipped over and sank again. Luckily it landed upright and he missed drowning. By this time he had enough and a yard crane ignominiously hoisted him back on dry land. Still, the test had not been a total loss. As Momsen told Watt, "You're wetter and I'm wiser."

He delayed putting the bell through its paces until he had concluded all the lung trials that culminated in his dramatic 207-foot ascent. Then more time was spent arranging for the mass production of the lung and in designing the lung-training tanks. A steel collar, meanwhile, had to be carefully constructed around the escape hatch over the *S-4*'s motor room to receive the grooved rubber gasket on the bell.

The strange contraption was sent by rail to Florida and placed on the *Falcon*. With the *S-4* in tow it was taken out to a shoal area about seventy-five feet deep in the Gulf of Mexico. A *Falcon* diver, once the submarine was on the bottom, attached the guide cables to eyebolts which had been welded inside the hatch collar. Then Momsen and Chief Torpedoman Charles Hagner, an *S-4* crewman, entered the bell. On the trip down through the clear water they could easily spot their target below. Landing with a thud, the two men were able to stand in about a foot of water on the deck, their bodies still inside the bell, and maneuver into position over the hatch without difficulty.

Now came the critical moment. Neither man said a word. They didn't have to; they both knew only too well that if something went wrong with the seal, if some flaw in concept or engineering had occurred, they would be dead in a matter of seconds. Theoretically, just by reducing the air pressure inside the bell, the sea itself ought to press them firmly against the hatch collar. To backstop them, Momsen had Hagner turn down four bolts he had devised to help hold the bell fast to the collar; at this stage, however, it was a problematical precaution.

Next he spun a wheel valve to let the air out of the bell, watching the water level with, as he later put it, "lively interest." But the seal was complete. The water level stayed stationary, and fog, caused by the drop in pressure of the saturated air, was still another indication that everything was all right.

His customary composure betrayed by a trembling hand, Momsen slowly opened the hatch on the *S-4*. He had warned her commander, Lieutenant Norman Ives, to expect some water and about twenty gallons ran into the hatch trunk. Then he looked down to find Ives staring back up at him. And despite all the work he had done with the lung, he was suddenly overcome by an emotion that left him speechless. But at last he pulled himself together and uttered the historic words never before heard beneath the surface: "Request permission to come aboard."

Ives selected two members of the *S-4*'s crew to be "rescued." The hatch was closed and the restraining bolts removed. Air pressure was admitted until it matched that of the sea outside, and with the seal broken the bell started up. Although this first demonstration was conducted under rigidly controlled conditions, the point had been made, the principle proved. The dream spawned in the days and nights after the *S-51* went down had finally been fulfilled.*

To perfect the bell, Momsen continued test after test. Once he arrived above the *S-4* to discover his twin down-haul cables had inexplicably crossed. Right then he decided that one such cable would suffice in the final design. Another time he took on a bigger load than usual and found the bell barely able to rise. This led him to the idea of portable ballast which could be dumped to compen-

---

* During this period at Key West, two more bell types were tried out and rejected. One, suggested by New York engineer John F. O'Rourke, was constructed from the remaining half of the *S-1*'s airplane tank. The O'Rourke bell had three anchors which were dropped in a triangle around an escape hatch roughly indicated by a marker buoy released by the submarine. The bell's operators then lowered it by turning hand reels that drew in the anchor cables. In practice, however, Momsen found it almost impossible to find the hatch, to say nothing of making a watertight seal. The other version was a completely closed chamber built by the Electric Boat Company. A sunken submarine released a marker buoy which was attached to the chamber. A windlass inside the submarine hauled it down to the hatch where the men entered it through an intermediate air lock. The principal objection to it was that the trapped crew had to do all the work.

sate for the additional weight of rescued submariners. The ballast would be sea water itself, carried in cans which the men who were being brought up could also sit on. The plan worked out beautifully except for one thing. As Momsen wrote in the dead-pan memo to the Bureau of Supply: "The ballast cans you sent have been received. The elaborate handles on their covers, however, detract materially from their utility as seats."

Twice he was nearly killed. It was felt that under certain conditions the bell might have to empty a flooded submarine compartment or at least blow the water down low enough for its operators to go inside. So the *S-4* settled down at sixty feet, her motor room flooded and the flood valves left open. Momsen and Hagner in the bell proceeded normally to the hatch. After the seal was made, the bolts were given an extra turn. Momsen was not sure how much pressure he would meet in the flooded compartment, but he suspected that it would be the same as the sea outside.

That was precisely the case when he started to open the hatch and he quickly increased his air pressure to keep the bell from being flooded, too. Building it up even more, he forced most of the water out of the compartment through its open valves. Then he and Hagner entered the motor room. In a real disaster they could have closed the valves or rendered whatever other assistance that might be required. Momsen sent a message over the bell phone to be relayed back down to Ives in the *S-4*'s control room that all had gone well. Ives could pump or blow out the rest of the water in the compartment as he desired.

But when Momsen and Hagner closed the hatch and tried to unfasten the bolts, they jammed. That was just the beginning. Too light to withstand the immense force placed on them, the bolt threads started stripping. If they pulled free altogether, the bell would soar to the surface. Swede Momsen never moved faster in his life. Instantly he reduced the air pressure in the bell, compressing the gasket against the hatch collar again and relieving the strain on the bolts. Then he and Hagner managed to wrench them out. On the way back up Hagner made a tactful suggestion. "Mr. Momsen," he said, "I think we ought to use heavier bolts."

Far worse was a later trial in eastern Long Island Sound, the *S-4* at 130 feet. For Momsen's companion, Chief Gunner Francis Church, it would be his virgin ride in the bell. Reeling down on positive buoyancy as usual, they were suddenly caught in one of the brutal currents that habitually rip through that part of the Sound. Even with the cable connecting it to the *Falcon,* the bell was swept away so that the down-haul cables were at an angle some fifteen degrees from a vertical descent. The extra strain caused one of the air motors to conk out. Momsen stopped the second motor to see if he could fix the first one. As he did, he momentarily took his eyes off the water level. When he looked back, it had already risen past the green warning stripe.

He upped the air pressure at once. But it was too late. The bell was falling on its own. And it had happened so swiftly that the crewmen handling the retrieving cable leading back to the *Falcon* continued to let it out. The deeper the bell sank, the more the air in the bell was compressed by the rapidly rising water. Momsen yelled to Church to be ready to get out if the bell turned over when it hit down. Miraculously, however, the bell not only missed the *S-4* by less than ten feet but also avoided at least a dozen boulders scattered on the bottom around them that Momsen could see through his glass eyeport. Thus far the sole injury either of them had suffered was the blood dripping from Church's nose because of the sudden change in pressure.

To his relief, Momsen found the bell's telephone still working. He asked the officer in over-all charge of the submarine safety tests, Lieutenant Palmer Dunbar, to transfer the retrieving cable to a capstan and to follow his instructions closely while hauling them up. It would be a ticklish operation. Momsen had to keep the bell this time at exactly the right degree of negative buoyancy or the whole business would occur in reverse. Then, just as they reached the point where the trouble had begun, the errant motor that caused it all abruptly started working. Momsen forthwith informed the Falcon to slack off on the cable, shifted the bell to positive buoyancy and reeled back down to the *S-4* to complete the practice rescue. "Anyhow, you've learned a lot," he consoled Church, "mostly in what not to do."

Despite such mishaps and some obvious design shortcomings, the bell in principle had been a huge success. The thing now was to improve on the original and a report incorporating the best ideas of everyone involved in the tests was prepared that would essentially transform what had been a diving bell into a rescue chamber. The new chamber had two compartments divided by a horizontal bulkhead equipped with an access hatch. The upper compartment would carry passengers seated on a circle of adjustable ballast cans, each holding seventy pounds of sea water which could be emptied as an equivalent weight of men came on board; it would also have a telephone, lights and fast-action valves for admitting and releasing compressed air. The lower compartment would include the air motor and reel for a single down-haul cable. Normally this compartment would be filled with water. If it had to be cleared, however, it was enclosed by a ballast tank capable of containing the same volume of water so that accurate buoyancy control could always be maintained.

Before Momsen could put these recommendations into effect himself, he was detached from the Bureau of Construction and Repair to train submariners in using the lung. Meanwhile Lieutenant Commander Allen McCann, who had arrived in Key West while the bell tests were in progress, was assigned to follow through on them.

When the revised rescue chamber was completed in the fall of 1930, Momsen and McCann tried it out in the same flooded dry dock at the Brooklyn Navy Yard where poor Watt had had his narrow escape. The chamber did everything asked of it, even landing on a symbolic hatch tilted thirty degrees and more. After this, it was loaded on the *Falcon* for a final check-out off New London. It was sealed and lowered to 400 feet for an hour. Next Momsen tested it on the *S-4*. Over and over he descended into swirling currents, cold water, discolored water, deep water and shallow water. Not a fault could be found with it. The chamber was pronounced fit and one was ordered for each U.S. submarine command around the world.

But there was an ugly twist to the story. Momsen in his stubborn drive to save submariners had stepped on too many toes, reddened too many faces, by-passed too many bureaucratic channels. Even the name "Momsen lung" had been a creation of the press; its official name was the Submarine Escape Appliance. This time no chances would be taken. Although Momsen had conceived of the bell, fought for it and personally pioneered its development, his life on the line much of the way, it was publicly unveiled as the "McCann rescue chamber."*

Nine years later, as he sat in the *Sculpin*'s wardroom, only a hint of the hurt he had experienced still tugged at him. What counted now was whether his baby could do the job.

---

* It is perhaps arguable that so many people were involved in the rescue chamber's final version that no one man deserves the credit. But as Captain W. O. Shelford of the British Royal Navy points out in his history of submarine rescue and escape, the one thing that made the chamber different from all other rescue devices was its motor-driven reel and down-haul cable which brought it quickly and directly to a submarine hatch. This, of course, was the key feature of Momsen's prototype bell. But Shelford understandably, if mistakenly, assumes that McCann was responsible for "this innovation." Indeed, the only published account I have been able to find accurately stating the case is an article in the *New York Times* on July 19, 1931, which noted that the rescue chamber "is largely the invention of Lieutenant Momsen."

He had sent diver McDonald to bed. If for some reason a quick descent had to be made, he would need all the rest he could get. Lieutenants Behnke and Yarbrough remained with him. They provided Momsen a special comfort. Behnke was matchless in his knowledge of the efficient use of helium and oxygen and nobody knew more about treating the bends than "Pete" Yarbrough. Momsen often worried that in their dedication to his underwater work the two doctors had jeopardized promotions they might normally expect by following more accepted paths to success as Navy medical officers.

As Swede Momsen pondered the past during those early morning hours of May 24th, there was something else for him to consider. Had the *Penacook* indeed grappled the *Squalus?* Or did the heavy manila line that was attached to the wooden grating bobbing in the black water outside simply lead down to some long-forgotten wreck?

In the Greenlee home at Portsmouth—the women drinking coffee, a platter of sandwiches left untouched—the mood had grown somber when the news came that at least some of the stern sections of the *Squalus* were flooded. The burden was heaviest on Betty Patterson. She knew perfectly well that her husband's station during a dive was in the after engine rooms. But she had never lost her composure. "She seemed to feel that Pat was safe," her sister-in-law Jacqueline Greenlee recalls.

Then, shortly after midnight, Frances Naquin, assured that the situation would remain unchanged until morning, asked to be driven home to look in on her two youngsters. As she walked slowly toward her front door, she found a cluster of newspapermen on the porch. Before they could speak, she said, "Please, gentlemen, I've had a bad day." The reporters left.

Mrs. Naquin entered the silent house, the children having

already been put to bed by the maid. She started up the staircase, then stopped and sat on one of the steps. At last, she thought, I can cry.

A few minutes later, the night quiet was shattered by the wail of police sirens. The rest of Momsen's experimental diving unit, following from Washington as soon as planes could be rounded up, had been forced down at Newport, Rhode Island, because of the weather. Transferred at once to cars as they came in, they were escorted northward at breakneck speed by successive waves of state police patrols. Now the first group of divers had just pulled into Portsmouth.

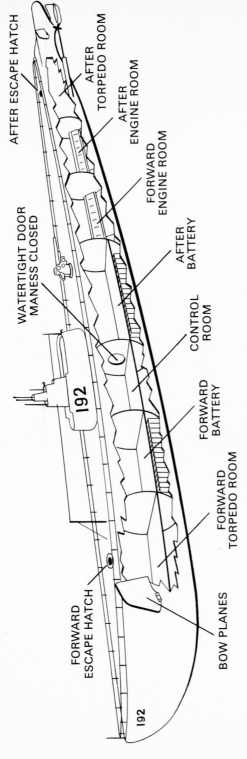

AFTER ESCAPE HATCH

AFTER TORPEDO ROOM

AFTER ENGINE ROOM

FORWARD ENGINE ROOM

AFTER BATTERY

WATERTIGHT DOOR MANESS CLOSED

CONTROL ROOM

192

FORWARD BATTERY

FORWARD TORPEDO ROOM

FORWARD ESCAPE HATCH

BOW PLANES

192

A simplified diagram of the interior of the *Squalus*.

Momsen as a lieutenant in 1930. (Wide World)

Momsen training submarine crews in the use of the Momsen lung. (UPI)

Momsen emerging from the water in a demonstration of the Momsen lung. (UPI)

One of Momsen's early commands, the *S-1*. Note seaplane tank on after deck later used for first diving bell. (Author's collection)

Escape hatch on the *S-4* through which man wearing Momsen lung would come. Note sealing collar around hatch for diving bell. (Author's collection)

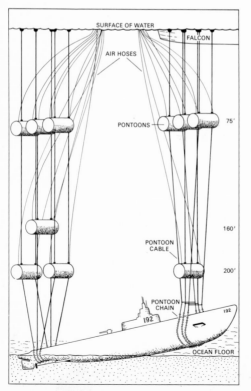

A diagram of the pontoons and their slings in the second flotation effort.

A *Squalus* diver in full gear,
wearing "helium hat,"
is seen on a diving platform
during the salvage operation.
(Author's collection)

A cross-section of the nine-ton
rescue chamber used to bring
the trapped men to the surface.

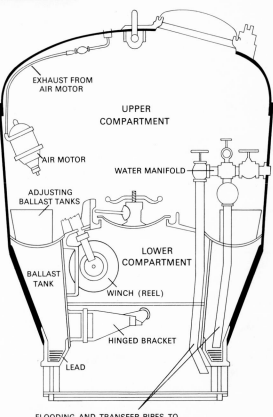

EXHAUST FROM
AIR MOTOR

UPPER
COMPARTMENT

AIR MOTOR

WATER MANIFOLD

ADJUSTING
BALLAST TANKS

LOWER
COMPARTMENT

BALLAST
TANK

WINCH (REEL)

HINGED BRACKET

LEAD

FLOODING AND TRANSFER PIPES TO
BALLAST TANKS AND LOWER COMPARTMENT

Momsen holding the lance nozzle
he devised to bore under the
stern of the *Squalus*.
(Author's collection)

Some of the Navy pontoons used in lifting the *Squalus*. (Wide World)

The *Squalus* shoots to the surface of the Atlantic bow first during the unsuccessful lift of July 13th. Moments later she fell to the bottom. (Wide World)

The *Squalus* at last being dragged toward drydock at Portsmouth. (Wide World)

Momsen as skipper of the
South Dakota during the last year
of World War II.
(U.S. Navy)

Rear Admiral Momsen commanding the Pacific submarine force in 1951.
(Author's collection)

7

Inside the *Squalus* those drugged into fitful sleep were
the fortunate ones. The cold had now become almost unbearable.
Huddled under a blanket in the forward torpedo room, Machinist's
Mate First Class Charles Yuhas stuck out a hand to flex his fingers
and quickly withdrew it; in a matter of seconds he could feel it
getting numb.

Nearby Harold Preble remembered how warm the forward
battery had seemed when he passed through it hours before. So
confident then of a fast rescue, he had paused by Naquin's
stateroom door, impulsively scribbled on it with a grease pencil
"Everything fine as can be expected," noted the time—9:25 A.M.
—and signed his name. He thought it would be a stirring reminder of the crew's spirit once they were brought up and the
Squalus salvaged. In the interim it had acquired a somewhat more
sardonic connotation. Still he could find a rueful humor in his
predicament. A fastidious man in work and habits, he had been
annoyed by bits of pineapple caught between his teeth after

supper; to clean them he had used the only item he was able to locate in the dim light—a sock left on the bunk he was in. But now he derived little solace in trying to divert his mind from the cold. What he yearned for most he could not have; Preble would have given just about anything for a smoke.

Rescue chamber or not, John Nichols never gave up hope of getting out of this mess. Despite the frigid waters pressing down on them and the rigors of an ascent through them, he was sure that most of the men had enough stamina to reach the surface with the Momsen lung. Besides the hasty primer he had provided Preble— the only man in the compartment who had not undergone escape training—Nichols carefully read aloud key precautions in the lung's use from one of the instruction manuals every submarine carried: be certain that it was right side up; hold your nose and blow hard to relieve the pressure against your eardrums; always keep breathing normally; never let go of the ascending line; once on the surface close the mouthpiece and flutter valve to lock in the remaining oxygen so that the lung could serve as a life preserver until a boat picked you up.

"If there are any questions," Nichols said, "let's hear them now." There were none. "Okay," he added, "the main thing is to conserve as much air as we can. We have sufficient oxygen on board so long as we don't start burning it up moving around or talking."

As he spoke, soon after the *Squalus* had settled on the bottom, Nichols first considered, then discarded, the idea of throwing in a little pep talk, the kind of thing a good football coach supposedly pulled out of the hat at half time if his team had been taking a trouncing. But such dramatics were out of character for him. And not once, as the long night wore on, did he have cause for regret on this score.

For Nichols the men under his charge in the forward torpedo

room were, quite simply, "a great bunch of guys." No one had shown the slightest sign of panic. Even Feliciano Elvina, the mess attendant who was so confused by the bewildering way the *Squalus* went down, sat calmly back going over everything he had been taught to do in this kind of situation. Elvina had a special worry. During lung training he always ran into trouble with the clip because of his flat nose; if he had to use it now, he reminded himself, it was important to put it as close as he could to his nostrils where there was less chance of its slipping off.

For some the common discipline that held them together required extraordinary will power. Jackknifed on a mattress he had dragged in from the forward battery, Electrician's Mate Second Class Gerald McLees was filled with a coldness that had nothing to do with the temperature of the North Atlantic. While many of the crew would have been routinely rotated to new stations for the afternoon dive, it was a little different for McLees. He wound up that morning, as it happened, observing how the forward batteries performed under the stress of a high-speed submergence— the same job his buddy John Batick was to do in the after battery. It had been left to the two of them, however, to decide who would watch which battery group first. Originally McLees was going to climb down into the after battery space. But in those last minutes just before the dive, when he saw that Batick had not finished the mug of coffee he was drinking, McLees grandly told him, "Oh, hell, I'll go forward for this one." Now he had no idea whether Batick was alive or dead. All he knew was that none of the men who had moved in from the control room remembered seeing him.

The two members of the *Squalus* crew of immediate concern to Nichols were Signalman Third Class Theodore Jacobs and Radioman Second Class Charles Powell, both sick to their stomachs and exhausted after having taken over communications with the surface. In response to a *Wandank* query at 9:15 P.M. to ascertain the placement of personnel, they had pounded back, again laboriously repeating each word three times: "Fifteen in forward torpedo room. Eighteen in control room." For two more hours, until Swede Momsen intervened, they continued to bang their hammers against the hull, answering requests for more information about conditions inside the submarine.

Although the *Wandank* called off further questioning, it was not until 1:55 A.M. on the morning of May 24th that she signaled: "Momsen says twenty-seven feet pressure will not be injurious." For the first time the *Squalus* crew learned that he, too, was now up there. Admiral Cole had been right. The name alone gave the men heart when they needed it most.

The forward torpedo room, as bad as it was, at least had remained free of water except for the one brief burst of the sea that shot through the overhead ventilation pipes when the long slide to the bottom began. But in the sodden control room—despite the double hull ringing it to protect its delicate instrumentation in the event of a wartime depth-charge attack—it was worse. For Lieutenant Walter Doyle the bitterness of the cold that had enveloped him, its relentless penetration into every bone in his body, surpassed the bounds of imagination. No matter what else ever happened to him, Doyle thought during those black hours, it was something he would never forget.

The cold had subdued them all. Long since forgotten was the whispered kidding, however lame, that helped ease the tension during the afternoon. "I wonder what they'll send down for supper," Seaman William Boulton had cracked. "How can you think of food at a time like this?" someone retorted. "I'll take a blonde instead."

Still a quiet defiance never deserted them. For Pharmacist's Mate O'Hara the *Squalus* not only was his first submarine but he had been on board her a sum total of twelve days. Under his watchful eye, young Washburn, who had been so severely seized by chills earlier in the evening, had at last fallen into a feverish sleep. Afterward Machinist's Mate Second Class Gavin Coyne, a strapping six-footer who had served in submarines for nineteen years, nudged O'Hara and said, "Sorry you switched to pigboats?"

"Don't bet on it!" O'Hara snapped back.

Even allowing for the stringent standards to qualify as a submariner, Chief Torpedoman Roy Campbell was astounded by the calmness that prevailed in the control room. Campbell was "Chief of the Boat," the ranking enlisted man on board the *Squalus,* on one hand Naquin's main bridge to the crew, on the other a sort of father confessor to any sailor who had a problem he might be reluctant to discuss with an officer. As such, he readied himself to step in at the first untoward note. But he had yet to make a move. Campbell just hoped it stayed that way.

Across from him Machinist's Mate Second Class Alfred Prien was consumed by a single thought. Almost as if he were facing a ghostly band of inquisitors standing beyond the shadows of the dim lantern light, he kept insisting in the privacy of his mind, "I closed the main induction valve. I pulled the lever as far as it could go. It stayed there. I checked the control board. None of the lights showed there was any trouble with the valves. They remained green until the whole board went out." As soon as the *Squalus* hit down, Prien had slipped a locking bar through the lever to hold it in a closed position. During supper, when there was a chance to move around a little, he glanced quickly at the lever to prove to himself that he was not dreaming it all up. "See," Prien wanted to shout, "it's closed!"

Lieutenant (j.g.) Robert Robertson couldn't understand it either. He happened to have been on hand when the induction valves were first installed and tested at Portsmouth. Then he was present again on April 30th, following the adjustments necessary on the big valve that fed air into the diesels. It operated, he recalled, perfectly—even better, if anything, than before. At the start of the dive that morning, the *Squalus* already dipping beneath the waves, Robertson had been inside the conning tower. Moments after word reached him that something had gone wrong, he heard the sound of air hissing out of the hydraulic supply tank behind him. Both main inductions were hydraulically controlled. Was this, Robertson wondered, the answer? Had the hydraulic system broken down at a critical point somewhere along the line? But this simply led him to a problem as perplexing. Why had the board registered green? Unlike the valves, it was electrically controlled. It seemed inconceivable that everything could have fallen apart at once.

In the cold dark one man came to a sober decision. Machinist's Mate Second Class Carlton Powell was as confident as anybody that every attempt would be made to get them out. But suppose help did arrive too late and the *Squalus,* like the *S-51* and the *S-4,* was eventually raised out of the depths as nothing more than a grotesque coffin for him and the others? Powell, who had unquestioningly stayed at his lonely post in the pump room throughout the awful plunge, was not a person easily rattled. He had to face up, however, to the possibility that these might indeed be his final hours on earth. If they were, he wanted to set things right. So Powell dug through hs pockets for a piece of paper to make out a last will and testament leaving all his worldly possessions to his wife. He paused briefly, thinking how to begin, before he started to write: "I, Carlton B. Powell, being of sound mind and body . . ."

Francis Murphy was grateful for one thing. Keeping the log at least helped a little to keep his mind off the intense cold. And shortly after he noted the *Wandank*'s signal that Momsen was on the scene, he added: "Men resting as much as possible. Spreading carbon dioxide absorbent."

This finished off the first can of CO_2 absorbent Naquin had ordered opened exactly twelve hours before. Determined to nurse his supply, he had a half-dozen cans to go. His first flask of oxygen, meanwhile, was about two-thirds empty. Like Nichols in the forward torpedo room, he had a reserve flask yet to tap. A fifth flask remained in the forward battery; he had decided to leave it there unless absolutely necessary because of the effort involved in moving it. All in all he reckoned he had enough to support life for another three days, perhaps longer. He could, if it came down to it, bleed air from the pressurized cylinders normally used to blow the ballast tanks. But this would build up the pressure they were being subjected to in the control room even more.

In his heartsick reliving of the dive, Naquin was no different from anybody else in trying to figure out exactly what had caused the sudden flooding of the after compartments. While he was almost positive that the sea had swept through either of the main inductions, it was still only a guess. But he had arrived at one firm conclusion. Both valves must have been closed during the initial phase of the submergence. Otherwise how could the board have been green, pressure evident in the boat, Naquin able to climb down from the conning tower, chat momentarily with Preble and then take his stance at the periscope before he felt that first warning rush of air? One of the main induction valves had inexplicably opened again after they were under. There simply wasn't any other answer that made sense to him.

None of this, Naquin grimly acknowledged, could begin to be resolved without the *Falcon*. Certainly it seemed obvious that those on the surface planned no more action until she arrived. Coupled with the *Wandank*'s message indicating a successful end to grappling operations had come news that the rescue ship would be overhead around three o'clock in the morning. Then, as midnight passed, the *Wandank* had signaled that this estimate had been changed to 4:30 A.M.

Naquin hoped there would be no more revisions in the timetable. He was deeply concerned about the effect of the cold on the crew. He had not pressed the matter in his own messages because he wanted to avoid creating any undue anxiety on the surface. For the same reason he also fudged on the question of whether either of the two occupied compartments were taking water by replying "negative" despite the leak Carlton Powell had discovered in the pump room. It had risen only two feet by midnight and showed no sign of coming in faster.

Now, with the cessation of the hammer taps, the control room fell silent, most of the men, as far as Naquin could determine, either actually asleep or resting quietly. Naquin kept himself alert by working out mathematical problems in his head. As soon as he solved one, he started in on another.

Around 2:30 in the morning he heard the beat of new propellers. His trained submariner's ears immediately recognized them as belonging to a destroyer. Although there was no confirmation of this, he was right. It was the *Semmes* bringing Captain Richard Edwards from New London to go over rescue strategy with Cole and Momsen prior to the *Falcon*'s arrival.

Then at 4:20 A.M. a new sound in the distance was picked up inside the *Squalus*. A crewman in the control room who had once served on the *Falcon* sat up. "That's her," he said.

In the first streaks of a bleak gray dawn, the sky still ominously overcast, Momsen watched her approach from the bridge of the *Sculpin*. The sister ship of the *Squalus,* like the other vessels set around the wooden grating through the long night, had backed away from it a minimum of 700 yards at Lieutenant Sharp's request to give him maneuvering room.

He would need every bit of it. Surface conditions could hardly have been less ideal for the task that confronted him. Spurred by a stiff wind, the vicious chop danced worse than ever off a heavy ocean swell that had suddenly developed, while periodic rain squalls swept in, reducing visibility at times to near zero.

Against this Sharp had to work the *Falcon* alongside the grating and straddle her securely over the presumed position of the *Squalus*. The initial plan called for him to lay out a four-point mooring, dropping four anchors in a rough square around the *Squalus*. Sharp began at 4:30 A.M. It took him four frustrating hours because of the wind and sea before he could spot his unwieldy charge between the anchors. Finally, when he did, it still was not enough.

At 8:40 the *Wandank* cautiously moved in, lowered a fifth anchor off the *Falcon*'s port beam and transferred the line to the rescue ship. Even with this, however, the *Falcon* failed to achieve the stability she needed; instead she continued to roll violently, her anchors already starting to drag, unable to hold fast as a shift in the wind now sent the swells smashing almost broadside against her.

Sharp, of course, could begin all over again. But the hours that might entail, when every minute counted, was something he would not accept. So after communicating with Admiral Cole and his squadron commander, Captain Edwards, he adopted a daring course. Personally directing the engine room over the speaker, he maintained a precise power while the bowline to one anchor and a quarter line to another were interchanged. Then he slowly swung the *Falcon* around so that she headed directly into the wind and waves. While this would not eliminate pitching, it was far preferable to rolling. More important, it secured her to the bottom. Sharp completed the maneuver at 9:45. As he did, both wind and sea perversely abated; even the cloud cover began to break up.

Swede Momsen, meanwhile, was preoccupied with preparations

of his own. Just before the *Falcon* showed up, his experimental diving unit—twelve in all, including Chief Machinist's Mate William Badders, who with McDonald shared the record 500-foot descent on helium and oxygen—had boarded the *Sculpin*. Along with them had come Commander Allen McCann, for whom the rescue chamber had been named, to serve as a technical aide on Cole's rescue staff. Momsen welcomed him cordially, holding him in no way personally responsible for what had happened.

Also under Momsen's operational control were the *Falcon* divers led by Lieutenant Julian Morrison. And before Sharp had started laying out his anchors, Momsen brought them over to the *Sculpin*, too. Since the *Sculpin* was a replica of the *Squalus*, he wanted each diver to familiarize himself thoroughly with her every detail. Thus in the gloomy depths, whenever one of them was on the sunken submarine, he would know exactly where he stood.

Now, with the *Falcon* in position at last, the stage set, the great drama about to unfold, a singular incident occurred which told you all you really needed to know about the kind of man Momsen was. Tension among the "hard hats"—as the deep-sea divers were called—was running high. They were a tough, proud bunch and an outburst of temperament in the natural rivalry that existed between Momsen's experimental unit and the *Falcon*'s diving team would be ruinous. So he had already determined to mix them up. There would be no bickering; each man was to have his turn. What's more, he would send a *Falcon* diver down first.

All this was quite understandable. But what set everyone back on his heels was Momsen's initial choice, a husky boatswain's mate named Martin Sibitsky. Sibitsky's diving career was then in the balance. A couple of months earlier, he had been recommended for disqualification following an attack of the bends in relatively shallow water. Momsen knew Sibitsky well, and when the report reached him in Washington, he couldn't believe it. He concocted an excuse for a trip to New London to look into the matter. After a discreet inquiry, he concluded that Sibitsky had been down much deeper than any of his superiors supposed, and managed to arrange another chance for him.

As Sibitsky sat back on the *Falcon*'s fantail, dressed in his cumbersome gear waiting for his helmet to be screwed on, Momsen simply said, "Skee, you know why I want you to go first."

"Yes, sir. Thanks very much."

"No thanks necessary. Just do the job I know you can."

Sibitsky went over the side on his diving platform and was lowered into the sea, deckhands on every ship around the *Falcon* silently lining the rails, the Coast Guard cutter *Thetis* in from Portsmouth jammed with newsmen, the sun picking this moment to poke through the clouds. At 10:14 A.M. he started his slide along the *Penacook*'s dragline.

Momsen kept in constant touch with him by phone. On air alone, without the revolutionary helium and oxygen mixtures, anything could happen going into these depths, even to the most experienced diver. Under extreme pressure, the excess nitrogen being forced into the bloodstream was capable of causing all sorts of aberrations. One man could suddenly feel gloriously drunk, another became morose, some completely passed out. Sometimes a diver suffered temporary blindness; often he was unable to distinguish left from right. No man, in any event, felt normal. Every act demanded intense concentration. A diver soon found that he had to repeat aloud to himself over and over again even the most elementary task given him.

Momsen vividly recalled an episode that had once happened to him during a practice dive at 300 feet. To all intents, his assignment could not have been more mundane: remove a cap from a pipe representing a submarine salvage air line, attach a fitting to the pipe and connect a hose: He took the cap off and put the fitting on by hand. Next he carefully repeated to himself, "I must tighten the fitting with a wrench." He located his wrench, set it around the fitting and began to turn it. But the fitting promptly fell off. Although Momsen finally realized that it was because he had been turning the wrench the wrong way, his attitude about the whole thing was total indifference.

Now, as Sibitsky reached 150 feet, Momsen called down to him, "Skee, how are you?"

"I'm okay," he said. "No problems."

At 200 feet he reported that he was still fine and that with the sunrays filtering through the water visibility was better than expected. He also notified Momsen that the dragline had turned sharply down. Whatever it led to was not far away.

Then he saw her, or part of her—the great dim bulk of the *Squalus* slowly taking form out of the darkness of the North Atlantic floor below him.

Momsen on the *Falcon,* Admiral Cole beside him rigid with anxiety, heard Sibitsky say, "I see the submarine." A moment later he reported, "I am on her deck."

"Where are you on her?" Momsen asked. "What do you see?"

Struggling to keep his senses against the tremendous amount of air pressure inside his diving suit to counter that of the ocean, Sibitsky first replied, "Just a minute and I'll tell you." Almost at once, however, he added, "Wait, I see the windlass. It is right in front of me. I am on the bow."

Momsen, his words slow and controlled, said, "Skee, can you see the hatch?"

On the deck of the *Squalus,* Sibitsky turned around and said, "Yes, I can see the hatch. It is right here." By some incredible miracle, despite the staggering odds against it, the *Penacook* not only had found the *Squalus* but had snagged her port railing less than ten feet from the escape hatch the rescue chamber would have to settle on.

As Sibitsky went toward the hatch, Momsen's old insistence that a diver had to spearhead any rescue operation, that it just couldn't be done blindly from the surface, was never more justified. Sibitsky spied a section of the broken marker-buoy cable lying directly across the hatch which would have blocked the seal the chamber had to make. He leaned forward and pushed it aside, even this seemingly simple act requiring enormous exertion. Then he notified Momsen, "I am on the hatch."

Momsen immediately told him that he would lower the down-haul cable for the rescue chamber. While Sibitsky waited, he stamped his diving shoes with their heavy lead soles on the hatch to let the trapped crew know he was there. Inside the forward torpedo room, already alerted by the *Wandank*'s oscillator that a diver was on the way, they heard each ponderous bang with breathless relief.

Seconds later Sibitsky saw the down-haul cable with its shackle glide into view, stop and dangle in front of his stomach. Like a man in a slow-motion film, he put his hand out to grab it—and missed. He shouted frantically. "I've lost it!"

Momsen, aware of the rising panic in Sibitsky's voice reacted quickly and calmly. "It's okay, Skee," he reassured him over the phone. "Don't worry about a thing. That was our fault. We'll get it right back to you."

Again the shackle came down. "Yes, I see it now," Sibitsky said. "I see it!" This time he caught the cable. Leaning forward until he was nearly prone on the deck of the *Squalus*, he connected the shackle to a ring in the middle of the escape hatch and reported that he was ready to come up.

It was 10:39. Sibitsky had spent twenty-two minutes on the *Squalus*. It took another forty-five minutes to pull him up in easy stages to prevent an onslaught of the bends. Only then did the cold hit him through his suit. For the thirty-year-old boatswain's mate it was a magnificent display of endurance and presence of mind under awesome stress. As he was hoisted aboard the *Falcon* and rushed into her chamber, Momsen whispered, with an accompanying wink, the Navy's traditional accolade: "Well done!"

At 11:30 the rescue chamber, or diving bell—as newscaster Trout would tell millions of radio listeners, "None of us reporters up here really know which to call it; officially it's a rescue chamber but it looks sort of like a bell"—was lowered into the water, its operators on this historic venture Torpedoman First Class John Mihalowski and Gunner's Mate First Class Walter Harmon.

Momsen, with McCann at his side, watched as it went over.* For the first time survivors of a sunken submarine were going to be taken out of their boat on the bottom and returned alive—and from a depth once thought unreachable. Not even this bell, ten feet high and seven feet across at its widest, had ever gone so deep in rescue run-throughs.

Tethered to the *Falcon,* it floated some twenty feet away, the lower compartment as yet unflooded, its main ballast tank and fourteen auxiliary cans now full, providing just enough positive buoyancy so that its gray top could be seen.

Admiral Cole had suggested sending a doctor along on the first descent. But Momsen, backed by McCann, dissuaded him. If the crewmen were that badly off, they would receive infinitely better medical attention on the surface, especially with the cruiser *Brooklyn,* delayed by fog most of the night, reportedly less than half an hour away. What ought to be delivered instead, Momsen counseled, were extra blankets, CO_2 absorbent, flashlights, hot soup, coffee and sandwiches.

Besides smacking of phony heroics, sending down a doctor

---

* Throughout the use of the rescue chamber during the *Squalus* disaster, Momsen and McCann worked closely together. As diving officer, however, responsibility for directing its operation was Momsen's.

meant one more man to be brought back up. There had been a great deal of discussion between Momsen, McCann and Cole about the number of trips necessary to get out the thirty-three men known to be in the forward torpedo and control rooms. The decision seemed headed toward five trips—four each with seven men, one with five—to keep from overloading the chamber. But finally Momsen decided to try for four. There were other risks to consider. The weather, although placid at the moment, remained unpredictable. Every additional descent, moreover, heightened the danger of some fatal breakdown, either mechanical or human. So seven men would be taken on initially to find out how the chamber operated with this load. He would increase the number to eight the next time unless the chamber obviously couldn't handle it. If, as he hoped, it carried them without difficulty, nine men would ride up on each of the last two trips.

Two minutes after the chamber was in the sea, Harmon announced that he and Mihalowski were ready in the upper compartment. "Go on down," Momsen told him. The air motor was turned on, and as the reel started winding in the down-haul cable Sibitsky had attached to the *Squalus,* the chamber crept along the surface like a huge water bug for perhaps a hundred feet. Then, blowing ballast while the lower compartment was flooded, it gradually sank from sight.

Inside the *Squalus* Naquin listened to the *Wandank*'s signal that the chamber was descending and that seven men would make the first trip. Over the battle phone, he instructed Nichols to pick, along with Preble, five men he felt to be in the worst shape. Nichols himself would go, too; Naquin wanted an officer on the surface for consultation if necessary. He and the rest of the men in the control room would stay put until the first group was out of the submarine. Moving into the forward torpedo room would simply overcrowd it and create confusion. There was one other thing. During the night the *Wandank* had requested the removal of all confidential publications. When Nichols asked about this now, Naquin said to forget it; it wasn't worth the waste in energy.

At 150 feet, thirty minutes into the descent, the rescue chamber paused. There was some trouble with the air vent lowering the pressure in the bottom compartment to maintain proper flooding and buoyancy. Three minutes later flooding commenced again. Harmon continued to sing out their progress until at last, peering through the chamber's porthole, he reported, "Submarine in sight."

At 12:12 P.M. the rescue chamber settled on the flat collar surrounding the escape hatch. Now the process that had begun on the surface was reversed. With Harmon and Mihalowski still in the normal atmospheric pressure of the upper compartment, the main ballast tank was filled while the lower compartment was emptied and the rubber gasket sealed to the collar under the enormous force of the ocean.

At 12:27 Harmon reported, "Seal completed." Mihalowski swung open the hatch dividing the chamber's two compartments and dropped into the lower one where, as usual, some water remained. First he attached the four steel bolts to rings around the hatch as a safety measure. Then he opened the hatch itself.

Up above, Swede Momsen heard it fall with a dull thud against the side of the chamber. "When I did," he later wrote, "I experienced a thrill I cannot possibly describe and I wonder whether any man ever could."

For a moment, however, he froze. "Upper submarine hatch open," Harmon notified him, "but no answer from submarine." What happened was that Nichols had kept the hatch at the other end of the escape tube closed until a drainage pipe siphoned the excess water, about a barrelful, off. That done, he ordered the hatch opened.

Mihalowski, looking down, could barely distinguish the pale faces staring back up at him in the dim light. There were no shouts, no cheers. Mihalowski himself was at a loss for words. "Well," he finally said, "we're here. I'm passing down soup, coffee and sandwiches." That broke the ice. "What, no napkins? he heard someone call to him. Somebody added, "Say, where the hell have you guys been?"

To go with him and Preble on this first ascent, Nichols had selected Isaacs and Fireman Second Class Roland Blanchard, the last two men to flee from the after battery during the desperate seconds before Lloyd Maness shut the control-room door. Next were McLees and Yuhas, both of whom seemed particularly affected by the cold. The fifth man would be Jacobs, who continued to vomit following his weary siege of hammering on the hull in the night.

One by one Mihalowski and Harmon helped them into the upper compartment of the chamber. After they were in, Mihalowski ran down an air hose and ventilated the forward torpedo room. At 12:56 Harmon announced, "Submarine hatch closed. Ready to come up."

Momsen ordered a thousand pounds of ballast dumped from the auxiliary cans to maintain positive buoyancy against the added weight of the seven passengers. Then he said over the phone, "Unbolt. Flood lower compartment. Blow main ballast tank."

Fourteen minutes later Harmon reported, "Seal broken. Coming up."

The chamber rose slowly, its air motor chugging away in reverse, the reel unwinding the cable hooked to the hatch cover on the *Squalus*. The seven survivors, dazed, said little. None of them had ever been inside the bell before and finally Isaacs asked if they were being pulled up by the *Falcon*. Mihalowski and Harmon explained how the motor and reel worked.

As the chamber neared the surface, it could be seen by correspondents in a half-dozen planes circling low over the sea. With about thirty feet to go, it looked to a New York *Daily News* reporter in one of the planes like a "great green blob." Then, suddenly, it broke through the slight swell, less than fifteen feet from the *Falcon*. Boat hooks quickly pulled it alongside and two sailors scrambled down to open the hatch. The time was 1:42.

Nichols was the first to stick his head out. A cheer went up from all the ships in the little fleet surrounding him. He blinked in the sunlight and faltered briefly as the ocean air hit his lungs. A dozen hands helped him stumble onto the *Falcon*.

Harold Preble, with whom Momsen had been having his stopwatch dispute, was next. He grabbed Momsen. The first thing he said was "Swede, I'll get some new watches to you right away."

For Momsen it was the culmination of his dogged efforts against the skeptics and thwarters, the result of all his work and planning to meet a hundred imaginary disasters. Commander Andrew McKee, an officer on Admiral Cole's staff who had been involved in many of his early experiments, asked him how he felt. "Numb," Momsen replied. He celebrated with a cup of coffee.

Something else came up on this initial trip, a roster Nichols carried with the names of the men known to have survived. When they were relayed at once to Portsmouth, the common bond that had united the *Squalus* women in the belief that all their men were still alive, frayed when they learned that twenty-six of them could not be accounted for, now disintegrated completely.

Earlier that morning pretty red-haired Evelyn Powell, wife of the machinist's mate who had written his will, rushed into the administration building and cried, "I can't stand this waiting much longer!" All anyone could tell her was to come back in an hour. Maybe then there would be some news. Mrs. Powell was just returning once more when she heard his name listed among the living. Tears streamed down her face. "I had almost given up hope," she sobbed. "This is the most wonderful thing in the world."

A few feet away Mrs. John Chestnutt, who had roamed for so long about the base before heeding pleas to rest, learned that her husband was missing. "It can't be so!" she screamed hysterically. "Last night I could see John's body floating around in that water out there. I prayed and prayed that it wasn't so."

In the pandemonium in the pressroom—reporters crowding around Lieutenant Commander Curley for more information, type-writers drumming away, phones ringing incessantly—the cruel paradox was enacted again and again.

Mrs. Robert Gibbs, in Portsmouth at last after her fear-filled train ride, simply stared blankly into space. A volunteer from the Navy Relief Society gently led her off.

Mary Jane Pierce, the five-month bride of Machinist's Mate Carol Pierce who had reported pressure in the boat as the dive began, couldn't restrain her joy. "When he left me to go on this trip," she exulted, "I told him I wasn't worried—that he was too ornery to die." Then she hastily interjected, "Please don't mis-understand me. That's just a kidding expressing we use around my home town of Kansas City."

Betty Patterson remained in seclusion in her father's house. Ensign Patterson's parents, flying in from Oklahoma, would learn of his apparent fate during a stopover their plane made in Chicago.

The tragedy went beyond the naval community into Portsmouth itself. Margaret Batick, the wife of Electrician's Mate First Class John Batick, had been born and raised there. Now, weeping uncontrollably, she was taken to the base hospital along with Mrs. Eugene Hoffman, whose husband had been stationed in the for-ward engine room.

Slim, blond Stella Hathaway, married two years to Fireman

First Class John Hathaway, also in the forward engine room for the dive, refused to accept the presumption that he was lost. She clung desperately to an announcement by Curley, "There is no final word about others. Nothing is definite."

So did twenty-year-old Ruth Desautel, the fiancée of Torpedo-man First Class Sherman Shirley. "He's too good a guy to be trapped like that," she insisted to newsmen in nearby Dover after they had discovered her wedding date was only five days away. "I won't give up hope until I am officially notified of his death."

These same scenes of anguish or rejoicing were played out in homes across the country as the news came over the radio. There was one dramatic exception. Somehow the names on the list Nichols had brought up with him did not include Seaman First Class William Boulton. In New York his wife, Rita, collapsed when she heard that he was "probably dead." Not for five grief-stricken hours would she learn that he was alive. Then she collapsed all over again.

Later, when the initial batch of blanket-wrapped, disheveled survivors arrived in Portsmouth on the *Harriet Lane,* the first man to step ashore was Charles Yuhas. Before he was hustled into a waiting ambulance, a reporter managed to ask him, "Glad to be back?" Yuhas looked at the reporter as if he had gone mad. "Yeah," he finally replied.

8

As soon as the rescue chamber rose from the *Squalus* with its first load, Naquin prepared to quit the control room. "Are any of you too weak to make it on your own?" he asked. When nobody spoke up, he took another precaution. By now the amount of chlorine gas in the forward battery was dangerously high and he ordered each man to rig his Momsen lung for use while passing through it. Over the battle phone he also instructed the eight men left in the forward torpedo room to put their lungs on until the transfer was completed. Then Lieutenant (j.g.) Robert Robertson cracked the forward battery door and they started moving out in single file.

Naquin was the last to leave. In the forward battery he paused in the passageway to open the hatch leading down to the batteries themselves. Just as he had suspected, his hand lantern picked up a thick greenish yellow cloud swirling toward him, and he hastily shut the hatch, relieved that the deadly fumes had thus far been contained.

In the forward torpedo room they all hungrily gulped in the fresh air vented in from the chamber. But despite this and the coffee and soup, the cold came at them again and they huddled together as before in a pathetic attempt to keep warm.

The chamber's operators for the first trip, Harmon and Mihalowski, were both from the *Falcon*. For the second trip Momsen replaced Mihalowski with one of his own men, Chief Machinist's Mate Badders. Once the switch was made, he promptly ordered the chamber to get going.

But now the barest hint of trouble developed. The clutch for the down-haul cable reel refused to engage and the chamber had to be lifted partially out of the sea to reach it. Only a couple of minutes were required to engage it manually, however, and the descent continued without further incident. Shortly after three o'clock that afternoon Harmon announced, "Holding bolts on. Opening submarine hatch."

Naquin waited inside the forward torpedo room until the excess water had drained off. Then through an eyeport in the lower hatch he saw the beam from the flashlight Badders was holding and opened the hatch. Naquin had already determined that he would send up the four remaining men—Washburn, Boulton, Bland and O'Hara—who had fought their way out of the after battery. As for the others, there didn't seem to be any obvious choice. Even so, the incredible discipline of the *Squalus* crew held. Not one man tried to catch Naquin's eye, to push himself forward, to claim special need. Each instead stayed quietly in place until his name was called.

Before the lower hatch was closed, Badders called down a cheery "Don't worry, fellows, we'll be right back." But it would not be quite that simple. When the chamber finally appeared on the surface, Momsen faced an unexpected—and bitter—decision.

It rode so heavily in the water that apparently the eight passengers he had scheduled to be brought up this time represented the limit the chamber could safely carry.

This meant—with eighteen men still in the forward torpedo room—the extra trip he had hoped to avoid. As if to confirm his foreboding on this count, the sky was clouding over once more, the wind building, the bleak North Atlantic starting to kick up ever so slightly. A dozen things might happen if the weather got rougher. For openers, suppose the *Falcon*'s anchors began dragging again? Momsen didn't want to think about it. Nonetheless he resigned himself to the inevitable. Turning to Cole, he said, "Admiral, I'm afraid we're going to have to make five trips after all."

Badders remained in the chamber for the next descent while Momsen put Mihalowski back on in place of Harmon. "Eight men," he told them. "That's it." There was some more trouble engaging the clutch, but at 4:25 P.M. the chamber went under. The rest was routine. Badders reported a successful seal and the third batch of *Squalus* crewmen ready to climb in.

At that moment in the forward part of the *Falcon* Lieutenant Commander Roy Sackett went goggle-eyed. A member of Cole's staff, Sackett had been looking on while blankets and coffee were being supplied to the second group of survivors before their return to Portsmouth. Something, he felt, was amiss. Suddenly Sackett knew what it was. Dashing aft, he shouted, "Swede, there was a mistake on that last trip. There weren't eight men in the chamber. There were *nine!*"

Momsen at the time could not possibly begin to appreciate the significance of Sackett's dramatic discovery. That would come, with stunning force, later. Right now only one thought possessed him. Over the chamber phone he quickly said, "Belay instructions regarding eight passengers. Take on nine, repeat nine, men. Tell the Captain to lean toward the lightest ones he can."

Up they came, the nine who would make the difference between a fourth and fifth trip, their ordeal etched on haunted, beard-stubbled faces, eyes red-rimmed, men chilled and weary beyond speech. But for Momsen they were as delightful a sight as he had ever seen.

Machinist's Mate Gavin Coyne set the pattern for them. Emerging from the chamber, Coyne struggled to maintain his balance, tottered for a second and fell back inside. Then deckhands from the *Falcon* reached down and got hold of him. Coyne sucked in a huge breath of ocean air. His throat burned. His head whirled dizzily, his back and leg muscles aching, as he was half carried onto the rescue ship. He felt as if he were coming down with the flu. His diagnosis was correct. Ten minutes later, however, he could say with a grateful grin, "Boy, I never knew the Navy made such good coffee."

Of the thirty-three men in the forward sections of the *Squalus* there remained Naquin, Doyle and six enlisted men. To get them out, Momsen now teamed up Chief Metalsmith McDonald with Mihalowski. As the chamber slipped beneath the surface for its fourth trip that long day, even the recalcitrant clutch, which had caused him some concern, engaged perfectly. On the average, each descent had taken an hour. Another forty-five minutes or so had been spent on the submarine. Coming up had been faster—around half an hour—as the chamber moved through progressively less pressure. Based on this, Momsen figured the whole thing ought to be over at just about nine o'clock.

It would be none too soon. It was starting to get dark. The sea continued to run higher; a few raindrops splattered on the *Falcon*'s deck.

By 6:30 P.M. on May 24th the first sixteen survivors of the *Squalus* disaster were bedded down in the Portsmouth Naval Hospital.

By then, too, the news that Boulton was in fact alive whipped the women whose men had been listed among the missing into a frenzy of renewed hope; if there had been one mistake, could there not be another?

But the first to feel the agonizing touch of uncertainty was Mrs. Lawrence Gainor, who had been so confident of her husband's safe return. She stood waiting when the cutter supposedly bringing him back pulled in. As she watched the rescued crewmen step ashore, her joyful expectancy slowly turned to fear. He was nowhere to be seen. "Where is he?" she cried. "Where's my husband?" Finally she saw him. The veteran Chief Electrician's Mate, his strength sapped at the outset by his heroic descent into the forward battery space was being borne toward her on a stretcher.

Now Ruth Desautel might have been speaking for everyone who had lost a man in the *Squalus* when she reiterated, "I can't believe it. I won't believe it."

The chance of an error kept Elizabeth Ward, the wife of Radioman Third Class Marion Ward, rooted in the administration building where, betrayed only by the constant twisting of her wedding ring, she struggled to hold her emotions in check. Uppermost in her mind as the chamber's fourth trip was announced was the knowledge that her husband's normal post would not be in the flooded stern sections of the *Squalus*. She was right, except that on this particular dive he had been assigned to the after engine room to record performance data.

Nearby the young bride of Machinist's Mate Second Class Elvin Deal, also stationed in the after engine room, tearfully approached officers and reporters alike with the same question, "Is it true they've heard new tapping on the hull? Oh, God, I just want to hear that he's safe."

After she had wandered off, however, all any of them could do was to shrug helplessly at each other. Bob Trout reflected their mood in his evening broadcast: "Here in the emergency news headquarters in the administration building, typewriters which have been pounding furiously for a night and a day are now hit lightly, slowly, if at all. Naval officers relax in swivel chairs for the first time and harassed reporters are beginning to think of shaves and clean shirts. For most of the story does seem over, the race against time won. Those who have been lost were lost yesterday morning when the accident happened. Those who lived have already been rescued or are coming up now, we are told, in the diving bell."

At that same hour in Portsmouth Frances Naquin arrived at the home of some friends. She had spent the day helping Navy chaplains comfort frantic wives, girl friends and relatives clustered around the Commandant's office. Now, at dinner, she listened to the compliments accorded her husband's leadership. Later she would leave for the wharf where he would be coming in. Then the phone rang. And again. Gradually Mrs. Naquin realized that the conversation was being led away from the *Squalus*. For a while she pretended not to notice. But at last, unable to contain herself, she blurted out, "What's wrong?"

"I'm sorry, Frances," her host replied softly, "but the bell has hit some kind of snag. I'm sure Oliver will be all right."

Out on the moonless, starless North Atlantic, floodlights glared down on the *Falcon*'s deck as Swede Momsen moved to meet a reversal all the more malevolent because it came just when everything was going so well, the sea seemingly cheated of victims it had long claimed as a matter of course.

The rescue chamber's fourth descent, if anything, was the smoothest yet. Exactly one hour after it had left the surface, McDonald reported that the hatch of the *Squalus* was being opened to receive the final group trapped in the forward compartments. Quickly the men climbed in. As tradition demanded, Naquin was the last to abandon his command, dogging down the hatch himself, noting as he did that it was nine minutes to eight. "Well," he said, "we're out of the boat."

At 8:14, the seal broken and main ballast blown, they started up. Then, with about 160 feet to go, it happened. The chamber abruptly stopped. Over the phone Momsen heard McDonald say, "The wire is jammed on the reel!"

There was more bad news. Under this unexpected stress the air motor that operated the reel conked out. Desperately McDonald and Mihalowski tried to coax it into kicking over again—to no avail. Next they resorted to a braking device normally used to control the chamber as it neared the surface. Increasing positive buoyancy while riding the brake might release the cable. But after rising perhaps five more feet the chamber would not stir another inch.

"We're stuck," McDonald said in a flat, emotionless voice.

Momsen made one more attempt to clear the reel. A second cable, called the retrieving wire, ran from the top of the chamber to a winch on the *Falcon*. "Stand by," he informed Chief McDonald, "we are going to heave on the retrieving wire." But this didn't work either; loose turns on the down-haul cable had allowed it to jump the reel and tangle beyond repair.

The only thing left was to unshackle the errant cable from the *Squalus*. To get some slack in it Momsen ordered McDonald to flood his main ballast. At the same time he had the retrieving cable played out. The chamber slowly sank. When it reached 210 feet, he instructed McDonald to hold it there.

Now somebody would have to descend into the black depths to finish the job. Momsen picked Chief Torpedoman Walter Squire, a powerful 200-pound first-class diver, to do it. Squire went over the side at 9:12 P.M. He slid down the same hawser Sibitsky had traveled that morning. Never was the fact that the *Penacook* had grappled the *Squalus* so close to the forward torpedo-room hatch more crucial. When he landed on the submarine, cold and groggy, fighting off the stupor of nitrogen narcosis, he bent to his task. But it was too much for him. "I can't unshackle the wire," he gasped. "It is too taut."

"Stay where you are," Momsen told him. "We will send you wire cutters."

Once armed with the big shears, Squire groped for the cable again and found it. On the surface Momsen listened to him grunt with exertion. The seconds passed. Then with savage strength Squire chopped through it. "I have cut the wire," he reported.

"That is fine," Momsen said. "We are bringing you up."

On the *Falcon* the first easy breath was taken since the reel had jammed. With the chamber swinging free, it could be hoisted to the surface on the retrieving-cable winch. The operation was started at once. From inside the chamber McDonald sang out, "We are at two hundred and ten feet. Going up smoothly." The ascent continued at a steady five feet per minute.

On the crowded fantail everyone watched the cable as it came over the side of the *Falcon*. Suddenly before their horrified eyes its individual steel strands began to unravel. The strain had been too great. Somewhere along the line they were parting. Momsen was dumfounded. They should have been able to withstand the pressure. And ordinarily they would have. But, unknown to him, he was not working with a single length of cable. It had been too short and an extra piece had been spliced on. Clamps used in the splicing had slipped and this in turn produced an uneven pull on the strands. Under such tension, Momsen thought, they must have popped down there like firecrackers.

While he had been apprehensive about a breakdown of some sort, he had not counted on one mishap after another. But there was no time to spare fretting over it. McDonald had last placed the chamber at 195 feet. To save what was left of the cable, Momsen promptly ordered him to flood his main ballast. He and McCann were in immediate and absolute agreement as to the next step: a diver would have to go down to attach a new retrieving cable.

It was now 9:30 and the eight remaining survivors of the *Squalus* disaster were right back where they started—on the bottom. The chamber's depth gauge read 232 feet. The men inside sat in a tight circle on the auxiliary ballast cans. Besides Naquin and Doyle, there were Yeoman Second Class Charles Kuney, who had been manning the control-room battle phone, and Machinist's Mate Second Class Allen Bryson, the forward-battery talker, neither of whom would ever forget the terrible plea to surface they had heard from the after compartments. Also huddled there were Seaman First Class Donato Persico, who had just missed being crushed by the dummy tin fish that went wild in the forward torpedo room; Machinist's Mate Second Class Carol Pierce, whose quick hand had triggered thousands of pounds of pressurized air into the submarine's ballast tanks in a futile effort to halt her sickening plunge; and Radioman Second Class Charles Powell, whom Naquin prudently had kept with him until the end in case additional tapping on the hull became necessary between rescue trips. There was, finally, the man who had sent up rocket after rocket during their long wait, Gunner's Mate First Class Eugene Cravens.

For the moment at least they were in no physical danger. The chamber was unheated and they still suffered cruelly from the cold, but they had light and a continuous flow of fresh air and communications with the *Falcon* were excellent.

The psychological stress of what had happened to them was something else. But Momsen would have little worry on this score. All through the early phase of the ascent and the subsequent jockeying to unsnarl the down-haul cable, they had been silent. Now, as the men awaited deliverance on the ocean floor, Momsen caught snatches of banter over the chamber phone. It centered mostly on steak and how each of them wanted it cooked when they were topside. Then to his amazement he heard Chief Metalsmith James McDonald leading them in a lusty rendition of "Old MacDonald Had a Farm."

As soon as Squire was back on board the *Falcon,* another diver, Torpedoman First Class Jesse Duncan, was lowered into the pitch-black sea to hook up a new cable. But as he followed the stranded cable down, he ran into deep trouble. Just above the chamber, his lines fouled in those belonging to it. The effort to untangle himself took every ounce of energy he could muster. Every time he tried, the new cable he was pulling down with his right hand would jerk him back up. Now the whole arm seemed paralyzed. "I am getting in trouble," he gasped. Duncan began to expel more carbon dioxide—or "smoke" as the divers called it—in his helmet than the ventilating system could handle. On the verge of passing out, he became incoherent.

Duncan had to be hauled up—and fast. As he was hustled into the recompression chamber where he would undergo the same pressure he faced below and be brought out of it in easy stages, he mumbled hair-raising news. The break in the cable was as bad as it could be. Duncan had felt it. All that remained was a single strand of steel about the thickness of ordinary string.

It was risky sending down a second diver who might wind up in the same fix. But the condition of the retrieving cable made it imperative. The risk had to be taken. The assignment went to Metalsmith First Class Edward Clayton. To give him a fighting chance Momsen ordered a thousand-watt underwater lamp lowered separately. During the descent, however, the lamp fouled in the stranded section of the old cable. Clayton kept going anyhow until he managed to reach the chamber. Time after time he attempted to complete his mission. There was a faint light coming through a small eyeport in the chamber's hatch but not enough to see what he was doing. In an extraordinary display of determination, he refused to give up. Squire, for instance, had spent eight minutes on the bottom and Duncan fifteen. Clayton had already been down that much and more. Finally, after thirty-three minutes, his own lines were tangling; his hands, through their rubberized canvas gloves, were so cold they lost all feeling, and the despair in his voice was increasingly evident.

That did it. Clayton had to be raised to the surface. And to send down another diver would be foolhardy. As it was, there had been two uncomfortably close calls with men of matchless ability trying to attach a new cable. If they were unable to pull it off, nobody could. Yet somehow those trapped in the rescue chamber had to be saved. Nor was there a moment to lose. There was a limit to what their nerves could endure and the weather, while not worse, wasn't getting any better either.

Momsen, after consulting Commander McCann, now decided on a bold maneuver. Addressing Cole, he said, "Admiral, this is what we want to do." The plan he proceeded to sketch was an all-or-nothing gamble. There was no alternative.

By having the chamber's operators carefully blow ballast so that it remained slightly below neutral buoyancy, the strain on the stranded retrieving cable would be minimal. Consequently it might still be used to haul the chamber up. But it would have to be done by hand. The *Falcon's* unyielding winch, rolling on a sudden swell despite her five-point mooring, could snap the last thread on the cable instantly. What had happened to the marker-buoy line was a stark reminder to them all.

It would require dovetailed timing. Once Cole's consent was obtained, Momsen got on the chamber phone himself to Mc-

Donald to brief him. "Whenever you get the word," he said, "I want you to blow ballast exactly as long as you are told. If you gain positive buoyancy, let us know immediately."

So it was, literally, down to the wire. Ten men took hold of it, Momsen in front, McCann right behind him, the starboard railing of the *Falcon* packed with tensely watching officers and sailors, binoculars at a premium aboard the cruiser *Brooklyn* and the other ships in the rescue fleet maintaining their distance 700 yards away.

At precisely midnight the slack in the cable was drawn taut and Momsen ordered McDonald to blow ballast for fifteen seconds. There was no response. He called for fifteen seconds more. Again nothing. It was absolutely quiet on the *Falcon* save for the sound of Momsen's voice. His only guide was the strain on the cable he sensed through his fingers. If he miscalculated and the chamber blew too much ballast, it would hurtle out of control toward the surface with every likelihood of splitting itself wide open as it smashed into the underside of the *Falcon*. And if he did not lighten it enough, that single strand holding the chamber would part, sending it tumbling back down, its fragile air hoses broken, the lives of the men inside snuffed out.

For the third time Momsen said, "Blow ballast fifteen seconds." He was, he felt, getting perilously close to positive buoyancy. But still the chamber did not budge as he gave the cable a tentative tug. Another fifteen seconds of blowing the main ballast tank would leave it half empty.

He ordered it. As he did, the strain on the cable seemed to ease. At a command from Momsen everyone in the hauling crew that was braced on the deck heaved up. The cable slowly came up over the side. The chamber had begun to move. The time was 12:04 A.M. on May 25th. One minute later it had risen four feet. It was off the bottom, suspended now at 228 feet.

The silence within the chamber was punctured only by Mc-

Donald's acknowledgment of each order to blow ballast and then
the rush of air as it was done. He and Torpedoman First Class
John Mihalowski, the broad grin that usually creased his face
gone, worked in swift, cool tandem in the cramped space of the
chamber's upper compartment as they operated the levers that
controlled its buoyancy—and their fate. After four minutes, the
depth gauge read 200 feet.

On the surface the waves were running some five feet. The men
hauling in on the line always went with the motion of the *Falcon,*
letting out a little whenever she rose, pulling in as she dipped.
Foot by foot the chamber rose. It was bitingly cold on deck but
Momsen could feel the sweat trickling down his back as again and
again they brought in more of the cable.

Suddenly out of the water right below him dripped the stranded
section. Momsen could see it glistening under the floodlights. He
watched it inch toward him. The temptation to give one last yank,
to get it over with, was tremendous. Then, all at once, it was over.
A deckhand was able to get a clamp around the cable below the
break.

The rest was simple. Steadily now they hauled the chamber up
and at 12:23 it bobbed to the surface. The long journey home had
been completed. The last of the *Squalus* crew to emerge from the
hatch was Naquin. Momsen stood by as he was helped to the
Falcon's deck. "Welcome aboard, Oliver," he said.

"I'm damned glad to be aboard," Naquin replied. Transferred
for the night to the *Brooklyn,* he went to sleep about an hour
later, his first in more than forty hours. Swede Momsen followed
him; he had not slept either.

In Portsmouth Hanson W. Baldwin, covering the story for the
New York Times, filed his lead for the late city edition. An
Annapolis graduate himself, Baldwin said it all. "Man," he wrote,
"won a victory from the sea early this morning."

9

{~}

THE HOPE THAT ANYONE WAS ALIVE IN THE AFTER COMPART-
ments of the *Squalus* was almost nonexistent. Naquin had reported
to Admiral Cole his conviction that they were all flooded with the
possible exception of the after torpedo room. And every attempt
to establish communications with men who might have taken
refuge there had failed.

But as long as there was a chance, however slim, it had to be
resolved. When Captain William Amsden, Cole's ranking representative at Postsmouth, announced that rescue operations had
been called off for the night after Naquin and the others reached
the surface, the outburst from frantic wives was such that Amsden
hastily denied it meant the Navy officially considered their husbands lost. If this were not enough, as the rescue staff gathered on
the *Brooklyn* in the morning to decide what to do, there was
among them, with a son-in-law still below, the forlorn figure of
Captain Greenlee.

Cole's order of the day was immediately flashed ashore: "Will resume rescue operations on after part of *Squalus*." In anticipation of this, new down-haul and retrieving cables had been installed overnight in the rescue chamber. Now, the sun shining brightly this May 25th and the sea smooth, the *Falcon* had to pick up and relay her moorings to position herself over the after torpedo-room hatch.

Then Momsen took over again. He had yet to send down officers as divers or chamber operators in order to demonstrate that enlisted men were fully capable of doing the job. But he felt that this was a perilous operation beyond the normal call of duty. For the same reason, whether officers or men, he would select only volunteers.

The first problem was to move the descending line aft so it could be used to attach the new down-haul cable. At that depth, on air alone, it would be a long, hard dive for Lieutenant Julian Morrison, who headed up the *Falcon*'s hard hats. Morrison was a particular favorite of Momsen's; as a measure of his affection and esteem, never lightly given, he nicknamed him "Joe Boats."

Morrison went into the water at 1:41 P.M. Three minutes later, on the deck of the *Squalus* near the forward torpedo-room hatch, he cut the manila line from the port railing, wrapped several turns of it around one arm and started walking it toward the stern. He reported good visibility in his silent world, perhaps fifty feet, as he passed the conning tower. His voice surprisingly clear and calm under 108 pounds of pressure per square inch, he notified Momsen that he had located the after torpedo-room hatch, observed the marker buoy in place and retraced his steps some fifteen feet forward to tie the descending line to the starboard railing.

It had been going so well that Momsen planned to send the down-haul cable directly to Morrison for shackling to save an extra dive. But the pressure on the young officer was beginning to tell faster than he knew. Morrison, under the impression that he was securing the line, suddenly discovered that he was simply waving his arms up and down, accomplishing nothing. He pulled himself together on sheer will power and began to knot what he believed to be two half hitches. "I have tied the line," he said.

Then Morrison momentarily blacked out. When he came to, he was astonished to see that instead of the two half hitches he intended, he had made turn after turn on the railing and followed them with a series of clove hitches before the half hitches. As he puzzled over this, he vaguely heard Momsen saying to him, "Joe Boats, stand by to come up. We are bringing you up."

But in his confusion Morrison went *under* the railing before he mounted the descending line and waited to be lifted up. "You are fouled," Momsen urgently told him. "Get back on the submarine." Morrison somehow sensed what was wrong, ducked back under the railing and, as he later dictated to a recording yeoman on the *Falcon,* "faintly remembered starting up again."

The next attempt to hook up the down-haul cable was a complete washout. A warrant officer, Gunner William Baron, reached the *Squalus* but when Momsen tried to speak to him there was no answer. Forthwith he was hauled up. Anyone whose ears have failed to adjust to atmospheric change in an airplane coming in for landing has some conception of the agonizing pain that Baron, at about eight times surface pressure, was experiencing when he could not clear them.

The third dive set everybody's nerves on edge. Boatswain's Mate First Class James Baker went over the side at 3:30 P.M. On the *Squalus,* once he got his bearings, he called for the down-haul cable. As soon as he had the shackle in hand, he pulled it aft with him. But Baker did not notice that the cable had looped around the descending line just above the railing, and the shackle was jerked from his grasp. He tried to follow it back to the descending line, but when he got there it had disappeared. As he had done with

Sibitsky the day before, Momsen quickly reassured him: "Don't worry, we'll send it right back to you. Make sure there is no obstruction over the hatch."

This time Baker carefully passed the cable outside the descending line and brought it to the ring in the center of the after torpedo-room hatch. Then he ran into more difficulty. Lying almost prone on the deck, Baker suddenly got the idea that the shackle pin, instead of being in the shackle itself, was hanging from it on a chain. With his breath coming faster as he vainly groped for the pin, his faceplate began to fog. He had enough presence of mind to stand up and open his exhaust valve one turn to clear it. Then Baker took another look at the shackle, finally saw the pin and started laughing at himself.

A worried Momsen was promptly on the phone wanting to know what was wrong. "Baker," he demanded, "are you okay?"

"I am okay," Baker said. "Don't take me up. I know what I am doing. It's hard to explain. It's just that the pin is in the shackle exactly where you showed me it was." A minute afterward he reported, "Down-haul wire fast to hatch."

Everything was now ready for the momentous fifth trip of the rescue chamber. In command would be Chief Machinist's Mate William Badders, his assistant Torpedoman First Class John Mihalowski. It was a descent unlike any of the others. Both men knew in advance that they were, quite simply, putting their lives on the line. Momsen went over the procedure with them. This time the chamber would not be able to make its usual watertight seal against the hatch. They had to work on the assumption that the after torpedo room was flooded, the pressure in there at least equal to that of the surrounding sea and possibly greater if it was topped off by a pocket of highly compressed, trapped air. Thus, instead of the atmospheric environment maintained in the chamber's upper compartment during the previous four dives, the pressure would have to be built up after settling on the submarine to match the expected thrust of air and water. All they could depend on to hold them to the hatch were the chamber's bolts. The slightest error in judgment would drown them instantly. And there was something else as hideous to think about. Once the chamber itself was pressurized, there was no way to exhaust the carbon dioxide the men would be exhaling. They would have to move swiftly; anything over twenty minutes, Momsen warned them, would be exceedingly dangerous. If they were overcome, there was nothing he could do to save them.

Badders and Mihalowski started down at 5:19 P.M. The initial phase of the operation was the same as in the earlier trips—flooding main ballast and blowing the lower compartment. Then, the chamber held to the *Squalus* by the down-haul cable alone, the air pressure in the upper compartment was steadily increased until it corresponded to the crush of the North Atlantic outside. Badders opened the hatch to the lower compartment and, ankle-deep in the water that always remained, he bolted the chamber to the *Squalus*. At 6:19 Mihalowski, manning the pressure valves in the upper compartment, reported that Badders was preparing to crack the after torpedo-room hatch.

He was doing it as gingerly as he could. But suddenly a rush of air exploded past Badders into the chamber. Right after it came the sea surging rapidly around his legs. "More pressure!" he shouted to Mihalowski. His partner reacted instantly. The sea hesitated, then fell back. Now Badders dropped to his knees and eased the hatch back until he was able to peer under it. But all he could see, level with the hatch opening, was water. The after torpedo room was completely flooded.

As Mihalowski relayed the news, Momsen sensed the woozy tone in his voice. The two men had been under extreme pressure for seventeen minutes. "Close the hatch," he ordered. "Come up."

Six more minutes ticked by before they began their ascent. It would take them two and a half hours to do it, following a decompression timetable supplied by Momsen. When they reached the surface, the greatest underseas rescue in history was finished.

For Swede Momsen, however, it was just the beginning. The *Squalus* had to be raised and returned to Portsmouth. By May 26th ugly reports were sweeping the country that sabotage had been responsible for the disaster. They were spurred by Machinist's Mate Second Class Alfred Prien's statement, during a press interview of some of the surviving crewmen, not only that he was positive he had closed the main induction valves but that he had checked the control board and "none of the lights there showed there was any trouble." Then the Chicago *Tribune* broke a story that a massive espionage search was under way in all Navy yards engaged in warship construction.

It got so bad that Captain Amsden was forced to declare: "Despite certain stories in the press, there is no evidence at this time to substantiate any rumor of carelessness or sabotage . . . the yard is spy-proof." Whatever good this did was lost when Amsden bowed to the demands of cameramen that Prien at least be allowed to pose for pictures the day after he made his statement. As the photographers clicked away at Prien, a reporter suddenly tried to interview him again. "I told you," the jittery Amsden shouted, "that Prien was not to be questioned! Do you want to get me court-martialed?"

Of far more concern to the Navy were the valves themselves. Although the consensus was that the big outlet leading to the engine rooms was to blame, it remained supposition at best. And even if it was so, was there some built-in defect? They had to find out. A sister submarine in the new class was due to be commissioned at Portsmouth in a few days, another would slide down the ways within a month, still more were in the works. Grief-stricken Captain Greenlee, as yard manager, put it as well as anyone could. "No one knows what really happened," he said, "because no one has gotten down there to see. Anything about the valves is mere conjecture. The cause of the disaster will not be known until the vessel has been examined in dry dock."

In order to get her there, everything depended on Momsen and his divers. It would be an unparalleled salvage operation, the *Squalus*—310 feet long, 1,450 tons—lying inert on the ocean floor, her hull partially buried in mud and clay 243 feet down, fifteen miles of open sea to be negotiated before she could be brought in. The statistics were staggering enough. But beyond this, in the ensuing struggle the giant submarine seemed almost to become a living thing with a baleful, sometimes raging will all her own. "Just call me Ahab," Momsen would wryly remark. He was only half joking. The *Squalus* once came within an ace of maiming him.

At first he privately doubted that salvaging her was possible. And without the helium and oxygen mixtures developed under his leadership while he was in charge of the experimental diving unit in Washington, it would have been hopeless. But an insistent fate had again placed him in the right spot at exactly the right moment. He had assumed command of the unit just twenty months earlier, in the fall of 1937. The move, as he then put it, was "most gratifying." It was an understatement. After the exhilarating experience of training personnel to use the lung and the rescue chamber at each of the Navy's major submarine commands, Momsen had languished aboard the heavy cruiser *Augusta,* flagship of the U.S. Asiatic Fleet—a tour of duty marked chiefly by heavy social demands for his expertise on the ukulele.

At that time the depth a diver could go to, the length of his stay there and the work he was capable of doing were all severely inhibited because he was being fed ordinary air, which, although we often don't think of it as such, is actually a gas mixture consisting roughly of 80 per cent nitrogen and 20 per cent oxygen. For a diver the culprit in this combination is the nitrogen.

If he comes up too rapidly after a descent, he will be hit by the bends. The name comes from the tortured shapes into which it can twist its victims. When a man is subjected to great pressure, not all of the nitrogen he breathes in his air supply can be exhaled. Some of it, instead, is carried by the blood into his body tissues in much the same manner that carbon dioxide is forced into carbonated drinks. As long as the pressure is decreased slowly, the nitrogen exits as innocently as it entered. But if the pressure is lowered too fast, it forms a froth of bubbles like a bottle of ginger ale that has suddenly been uncapped. These bubbles tend to concentrate at the bone joints. The pain even in a mild attack is excruciating. In a severe case the bubbles clog the veins completely and can cause instant death from heart embolism.

Still more insidious during a deep dive is the way nitrogen attacks the central nervous system and drastically affects neuromuscular coordination. Initially its narcotic effect gives a diver a giddy, almost drunken sense of well-being. Eventually, along with a carbon dioxide build-up inside his helmet, it knocks him out.

Thus, simply stated, the problem that confronted Momsen and his dedicated medical team was to come up with some substitute for nitrogen or find some means to counter its action so that a diver could go deeper than ever before, remain alert throughout his mission and return as speedily as possible to the surface. It was a good deal easier said than done.

Oxygen, which does not bubble up in the bloodstream during decompression, was an ideal answer as far as the bends were concerned. But under pressure it, too, has a sinister quality. At a depth of around sixty feet, even for the most experienced diver, pure oxygen becomes abruptly and dangerously toxic. His lips begin to tremble, his eyelids flutter; within seconds he is blind and in the grip of terrible epileptic-like convulsions. The reason oxygen could be used safely to inflate Momsen's artificial breathing device was that a man wearing one started out with a lungful of air. Since he was also coming straight up in a matter of minutes, constantly decompressing, the oxygen in the bag merely replenished his initial supply.

Helium, which is found almost exclusively in the United States, first attracted attention for diving in 1925. The Navy even looked into its potential for a while, but the project, not very extensive to begin with, petered out. Under Momsen the investigation was revived in earnest. The earlier experiments had indicated that helium might be an improvement over the high nitrogen content in air. On the other hand it had been demonstrated that it was no panacea; a diver could get the bends just as badly, if not worse, from a helium and oxygen mixture as from air. So, with Drs. Behnke and Yarbrough working tirelessly at his side, Momsen strove to piece together a definitive picture of helium's impact on diving physiology.

From the beginning it was tough, tedious, often disheartening going, especially in terms of decompression, the big pressure tank at the Washington Navy Yard a daily chamber of horrors as diver after diver suffered the bends. The name of the game was the educated guess, an intuitive move, endless trial and error. As with his previous underwater work, there was practically nothing to fall back on. Up until then, for example, the most notable testing in this area had been conducted by the British, who tried a blend of half helium and half nitrogen, along with enough oxygen to support life. The theory was that the two gases would act independently of each other after entering the body; if this was so, the decompression schedule could be keyed to either the helium or the nitrogen, thus halving the time required to bring a diver up. When nothing of the sort happened, the British concluded that there was no point in using helium for deep diving. "Had they," Momsen noted in his log, "pursued their inquiry and tried helium with oxygen alone, they would have discovered its real value, that of clear and comfortable thinking under pressure."

Still, before he could demonstrate this, all kinds of pitfalls lay ahead. In his tenacious odyssey through the mysterious forces that affect man beneath the surface of the sea, Momsen even attempted a variation on the British theme. Divers were given a helium and oxygen mix for twenty minutes and then were switched to air for another twenty minutes. The hope was that the helium, which is considerably lighter than nitrogen and has a much higher diffusion rate, would be eliminated from a diver's body during the time air was being administered to him. Hence only the nitrogen in the air had to be taken into account in his decompression. If it worked, it would mean that a diver could stay down for hours alternating between helium and oxygen and air with a decompression period for just the final twenty minutes he was on air. But it didn't work; the bends always followed.

Momsen refused to give up. For months other approaches were painstakingly explored—without success. All the testing, however, was not a complete waste. In the end he became convinced that no matter how many gases were juggled around to create a breathing mixture with oxygen, they all had to be taken into consideration in decompression. Out of this he settled on his fundamental proposition: First, to use helium to maximum advantage, only helium and oxygen should be fed to a diver on the bottom. Second, to keep the amount of helium absorbed in his body to a minimum, the percentage of oxygen must be as great as possible.

A simple experiment dramatically showed the superiority of this combination over air deep in the sea. A yeoman attached to the unit was placed under pressure at a simulated depth of 200 feet with his typewriter. He was first given air for five minutes while he copied a standard typing exercise. Next he repeated the exercise for five more minutes on helium and oxygen to see what effect it would have on his coordination of mind and muscle. Momsen was a bit jolted when the yeoman said that he was sure he had done better on air. Quite the opposite, in fact, was true. Breathing air under pressure had lulled him into a false sense of security which drastically impaired his judgment. While breathing helium and oxygen, however, he was much more alert and knew exactly when he had struck a wrong key. The number of words he had copied in each instance was about the same, but he had made three times as many mistakes, even skipping entire lines, on air without being aware of it.

Once this had been established, finding a way to bring up a diver safely and speedily still plagued Momsen. Every attempt to shorten the decompression time again resulted in divers being viciously hit by the bends. Finally he returned to the old rates of ascent used for a diver who had been on air. But to his consternation it didn't seem to make much difference; there was still an alarming number of men who developed the bends and it was becoming a serious morale problem. Obsessed by an unknown factor that suddenly threatened to wreck the whole project, his medical people as mystified as he was, Momsen angrily headed each night's computations in his notebook: "What the hell am I doing wrong? What does helium do that nitrogen doesn't?"

He awoke early one morning with the answer. A diver on air starts his long, dreary ascent with comparatively brief decompression stops that increase in duration as he nears the surface. The trouble, Momsen was sure, must be at the first stop. Helium, with its high diffusion rate, rushed out of a diver's body tissues so much aster than nitrogen that his bloodstream did not have time enough to cope with the load, and bubbles formed which brought on the bends. By fixing the initial stop of a man coming up after a helium and oxygen dive at never less than seven minutes, the incidence of bends at once dropped almost to zero.

This was capped by another break-through that spectacularly cut the time a decompressing diver had to stay in the water. In an exhaustive study of human tolerance to oxygen under pressure Dr. Behnke had discovered that shifting a man to pure oxygen once he reached fifty feet and was past its toxic stage not only prevented bubbles from forming but actually hastened the elimination of excess helium in his system. This meant that a diver after his first stop could be raised fairly quickly to fifty feet. Next, instead of letting him dangle in the sea at that point, he would be hauled directly to the surface, hustled into a recompression chamber and fed pure oxygen at a pressure equal to the fifty-foot depth he had just left.

A great deal of work remained—all the calculations, as complex as they were vital, to establish new physiological diving norms, to plot the limits of human endurance, to determine the most efficient helium and oxygen ratios. But it had become a matter of refinement; there were no more blind alleys to follow or seemingly impossible hurdles to leap.

Divers could chuck for good the old saws—always eat an apple prior to a dive, eat nothing at all the day of a dive, don't drink liquor the day before a dive—they used to devise, like roulette players trying to beat the system, to ward off the bends. With the simulated descent of Badders and McDonald to 500 feet—the structural limit of the pressure tank—deep-sea diving was put on a rational footing never before achieved.

It also caused the first major innovations in diving dress, which had stayed essentially the same during the hundred years since a German-born inventor named Augustus Siebe, who settled in

England, devised his prototype suit. Divers on air often suffered terribly from the cold. Helium, however, was far worse. Body heat dissipated through it so rapidly that a water temperature of about sixty degrees was all a man could endure for very long. Yet in the depths opened up by helium and oxygen, freezing temperatures would be commonplace. Momsen took his problem to a New York manufacturer who was turning out electrically heated clothing for pilots flying at high altitudes. The result was special underwear with wired pads sandwiched between two layers of wool. But with so much oxygen involved, Momsen also wanted protection against the ghastly possibility of fire and he had just received a new batch of the electric long johns with the wiring wrapped in glass thread insulation.

These same depths made the build-up of carbon dioxide more dangerous than ever. While carbon dioxide in small doses isn't particularly harmful on the surface, its effect increases in proportion to the depth, finally triggering a cruel process of asphyxiation that divers call "the chokes." The kind of open ventilation system in which an endless supply of air can be sent down to a diver and expelled into the sea was out of the question since a synthetic blend like helium and oxygen could be stored only in limited quantities aboard ship. This led Momsen to the creation of the "helium hat." Unlike air helmets, it formed a single unit with a diver's breastplate to prevent gas leakage. Inside it featured an ingenious recirculating device which sucked the helium and oxygen through a container of CO_2 absorbent and then forced it back into the main supply line. Although the helium hat was still in the experimental stage when the *Squalus* went down, it was far enough along to show it was capable of reducing by 80 per cent the amount of helium and oxygen that would otherwise be required.

So in a scant twenty months the art of diving deep into the sea, all its concepts and potential, had been completely revolutionized. For Momsen it opened up an almost bottomless vista. "Suddenly," he wrote at the time, "we have actually projected the depth at which man may work efficiently and safely to 500 feet and theoretically to a thousand feet, bringing within human grasp more than a million square miles of the earth's surface with an incredible storehouse of natural treasures as yet untouched. It is just the beginning. Surely the day must come when man will lay claim to vast expanses of what we call the high seas."

But now, without warning, instead of the leisurely summer of 1939 he had planned to spend off Portsmouth proving out his controlled laboratory work, all of it—the helium hat, the heated diving suits, the use of oxygen in decompression, the whole development of the new breathing mixture as a substitute for air— faced a crucial test.

10

ON JUNE 1ST, NINE DAYS AFTER THE *Squalus* HAD PLUNGED TO the bottom, the magnitude of everything Swede Momsen had done became tragically apparent. A new British submarine, the *Thetis*, on her virgin dive sank a few miles off Liverpool because of a faulty sea cock in a bow torpedo tube. On board, besides her regular crew, were a large number of guests and observers, 103 men in all. But although she was just 150 feet down with her stern sticking out of the water, only four of them escaped. The rest either drowned or suffocated.*

By then efforts to salvage the *Squalus* were already under way. The over-all plan called for heavy chains to be slipped under her bow and stern. Cables from these chains would be attached to a

---

* Error after error compounded the *Thetis* disaster. Three particularly stand out. First, surface help was slow to organize and once on the scene was almost criminally ineffective. Second, while escape lungs were available to the trapped crewmen, they had no training in their use at depths of more than fifteen feet. (The U.S. training towers were dismissed as typical "American showing off.") Third, the *Thetis* had no carbon dioxide absorbent and thus no way to stave off its deadly build-up during the period when escape was still possible.

number of big lifting pontoons. Hoses, meanwhile, were to be connected to her fuel tanks to pump them dry. Still others would run to all ballast tanks and flooded compartments to clear them of water with compressed air.

On paper it looked good. But while Momsen concurred in principle, he felt that Admiral Cole and his senior aides were wildly optimistic in their belief that the job could be completed in a couple of weeks. He was particularly disturbed by the excessive diving assignments being scheduled, some of which required actual entry into the submarine.

The first day's diving, on May 26th, was enough to sober everyone. Although the helium and oxygen mix had not yet arrived from Portsmouth, Momsen was anxious to have a permanent descending line on the *Squalus* before something happened to the temporary one used in the rescue phase of the operation. Six-inch manila hemp ought to do it, he thought, without being too large for a diver to ride. So he sent down on air Joseph Alicki and Forrest Smith, both boatswain's mates and expert riggers, to fasten it to the main gun on the afterdeck. Once Alicki and Smith reported they were on the submarine, the new line, weighted and shackled to the old one, was dropped. When it reached them, Alicki grabbed the end and started to crawl toward the gun, requesting the *Falcon* to tell Smith to give him more slack. Not getting any, he turned around and saw his partner slumped on the deck. Alicki let go of the line, slid back to Smith, checked his control valve to make sure he was receiving air and then began shaking him. Smith, in the throes of nitrogen stupor, later recalled "being awakened from a deep sleep." The first thing he saw was the new line dangling about four feet from the submarine. He tried to help Alicki retrieve it but Momsen, by now thoroughly alarmed, ordered them up. Alicki went first. As Smith followed, he passed out again. The next thing he knew, Alicki was pulling him onto their diving stage, the big metal platform which lowers divers into the water and lifts them out again.

Afterward Momsen had the new descending line hauled in; for the time being he would settle for a more manageable four-inch line. To secure it to the gun he called on the *Falcon*'s master diver, Chief Boatswain's Mate Orson Crandall. But no sooner had Crandall touched down than he was also overcome by the narcotic action of the nitrogen in his air supply. Under the illusion that he was reporting a safe landing on the *Squalus,* he was in fact babbling nonsensically over the phone and was brought up forthwith. All he remembered before losing consciousness was being "jerked off the submarine." When he came to, Crandall found himself jammed underneath the diving stage. Gasping out his predicament, he was finally given enough slack in his lifeline to climb on it.

That ended diving for the day. It could not have been a more inauspicious beginning. Momsen, masking his own disappointment, moved quickly to buck up the divers. As they gathered around him on the *Falcon,* he blithely declared that "those damn gnomes below" were to blame.

There was a pause before one diver said, "How do you spell that, sir?" When Momsen obliged, the diver's face lit up. "Oh," he said, "you mean ganomes." Momsen didn't argue the point. From then on the "ganome" became an integral part of their daily vocabulary, to be cursed at or joked about, the perfect scapegoat for anything that went awry. The word spread through the Navy. Later, in odd parts of the world, Momsen would invariably meet somebody who asked him just what a ganome was. He had a stock answer to perpetuate the legendary creature. "Oh," he would say, "it was a special kind of devilfish we encountered off Portsmouth."

The well-being of his divers was Momsen's overriding concern.

Whether on air or helium and oxygen, they still faced terrible perils. In the maze of hoses and lines that would gradually festoon the *Squalus*, a man could easily cut his own breathing supply by mistake. Groggy from too much exertion, he might open his pressure-control valve too far and "blow up" his suit, soaring to the surface in a matter of seconds, dead or perhaps crippled for life. Worse yet, should he fall off the submarine, he could wind up in the fearsome grip of what divers called "the squeeze." It was a literal description. Pressure in a helmet must always be equal, within a few ounces, to that of the surrounding sea. In a sudden fall—every two feet of which added another pound of pressure per square inch—a diver had to adjust to it instantly. If he didn't, the squeeze began first in his feet and then coursed irresistibly up his body until he was finally stuffed inside his own helmet.

A loudspeaker system was rigged on the *Falcon*'s deck so that Momsen remained in constant earshot of every man on the bottom. Each diver was required to report continuously over his phone—if nothing specific, simply that he was "okay." Failure to do this, the slightest indication of erratic behavior, immediately brought forth the order "Stand by to come up." It was to be obeyed without question.

Instilling absolute confidence among the divers in surface authority was equally important. "No diver is to be bawled out, criticized or corrected while in the water," he informed his deck crew. "I especially don't want to hear one telephone talker ever raising his voice or showing any sign of impatience or excitement. Nor do I expect to hear of a diver being criticized even after he is up. If he fails an assignment, he'll be miserable enough as it is without somebody else telling him about it."

In all, Momsen had fifty-eight divers, three of them masters, most of the rest rated first class and qualified at least at 200 feet, as well as a scattering of second class men who had not been deeper than ninety feet. They came from his experimental unit, the diving school in Washington, the *Falcon,* the submarine base at New London and assorted other commands. Many were strangers to him and detailing them was a ticklish business. Still, it was essential that everyone had his fair share of dives, not only because of pride but also because of the bonus pay involved. In the end he mixed them up as judiciously as possible into three sections, four days on duty and two off, each with the same percentage of less experienced men whom he would gradually work into the diving routine.

Momsen, beyond his exploits with the lung, the rescue chamber and the use of helium and oxygen, had an extra plus going for him to hold the unswerving loyalty of these hard-bitten men who went into the sea. When the old *S-51* sank in 1925, a number of supposedly qualified divers turned out to be worthless. By the time the *S-4* went down two years later, little had been done to improve the situation. Momsen even discovered one man listed as a diver who had never been inside a diving suit. That did it. In 1929 all first class divers were automatically disqualified. The only way they could regain their rating was to pass a completely revamped training program. The first commissioned officer in the Navy to graduate from it was Swede Momsen.

A diver, interviewed during the *Squalus* salvage by Harold Bennison of the Boston *Traveler,* explained just how they felt about him. "On the bottom," he said, "Mr. Momsen is right there with you. When you know that, you ain't working one hand for the government and one hand for yourself like we always say. It's both hands for the Swede."

Momsen would need every bit of their devotion. After the first day's futile attempt to attach a permanent descending line, setback followed setback. Bubbles had been spotted coming out of the main engine air-induction valve which definitely established, for whatever reason, that it was open. A try at manually closing its twin on the *Sculpin* from the outside proved so difficult that the idea of doing it in the depth the *Squalus* was in had to be abandoned. This made it impossible to pump out the four flooded after compartments and eliminated any chance of lifting her all the way to the surface at once. With such uneven weight distribution, she would simply be too unmanageable. Instead, a series of short lifts had to be executed while the *Squalus* was towed into shallower water.

Then two motor whaleboats under the direction of Commander McCann went out to see if they could maneuver a cable under the bow of the submarine from the surface as a prelude to placing a pontoon chain under it. They succeeded all too easily—on their first pass. While this meant that the chain could be slipped around without difficulty, it also indicated that the stern must be deeply buried in mud and clay.

Worse yet was the performance of the vital helium hat. After its arrival, Gunner's Mate First Class Louis "The Greek" Zampiglione made the initial descent to the deck of the *Squalus* wearing it, remained there for thirty-three minutes and reported it working perfectly, the electrically heated underwear fulfilling every hope and no sign whatever of the drunken, groggy sensation that a man on air habitually experienced.

But Momsen's delight was short-lived. In ensuing dives the recirculator that sucked helium and oxygen through the CO_2 absorbent malfunctioned badly, making the flow of gas ominously irregular. "I should have known better," Momsen ruefully muttered to Lieutenant Thomas Willmon, who with Behnke and Yarbrough rounded out his medical team. Throughout all the helium and oxygen experimentation in Washington, Zampiglione had emerged as some sort of physiological freak who drove everybody crazy in trying to come up with reliable diving norms.

He seemed totally immune to the bends and it had gotten to the point where no test in the pressure tank involving Zampiglione could be chalked up as a success until another diver duplicated it.

Momsen decided there was no way out. The helium hat was essential to salvaging the *Squalus* and it had to be returned to Portsmouth for extensive rechecking of the circulation system. Divers, meanwhile, would have to keep going down on air. But while nitrogen narcosis was to be expected at 243 feet, its intensity surprised them all. Dr. Behnke had the answer. "Swede," he said, "I don't think we're getting the carbon dioxide out of the helmet fast enough. Apparently it's augmenting the effect of the nitrogen." So the diving manual, which specified 180 pounds of pressure at the depth they faced, was shelved. To increase ventilation Momsen upped the pressure on a diver's air lines to 250 pounds per square inch. It was a makeshift solution, but it helped.

By June 5th, after fifty-eight dives, a total of three descending lines had been secured to various parts of the *Squalus,* compressed air had been introduced into each of the three forward compartments to keep them free of water and air hoses were attached to all the after ballast tanks. While the helium hat continued to be worked on, Momsen had set up a temporary rack of twenty helium and oxygen cylinders on the *Falcon* which could supply a diver wearing a regular air helmet. This entailed a tremendous waste of the synthetic mix and only a limited number of dives could be made with it on a given day.

Incredibly, there had just been one really bad moment thus far. Torpedoman First Class John Thompson suddenly lost his grip on the descending line he was following down to the *Squalus.* Over his phone, before the deck crew could react, came the dreaded words "I am falling!" But Thompson was lucky. Still conscious as he hit the bottom, he was able to give himself a "shot" to meet the abrupt increase in pressure that might have squeezed him to death.

Up till now, however, everything had been child's play compared to what lay ahead. The stern of the *Squalus* turned out to be embedded fully eighteen feet into the North Atlantic bottom. Momsen vetoed all suggestions that divers tunnel beneath it. At that depth it was far too dangerous. Instead, he designed a miniature nozzle similar to the kind used in tunneling. Six-foot lengths of pipe, bent to the curvature of the submarine's hull, would be added to it while the *Falcon* pumped down water through a high-pressure hose to blast an opening in the mud and clay so that first a cable and then pontoon chains could be passed around her tail.

Commander Andrew McKee, the senior Construction Corps officer on Cole's salvage staff, promptly put Portsmouth to work on it, and "the lance," as it was soon dubbed, arrived on board the *Falcon* on June 5th. It got off to a splendid start. The first diver down, Torpedoman Second Class Adrian Vanderheyden, maneuvered the first two sections of pipe into position in jig time. But after the hose had been removed to connect the next section, five divers in a row, including rated masters like McDonald and Badders, failed to do it primarily because the motion of the *Falcon* in a choppy sea so affected the hose that it was impossible to line up the fitting.

The next day, the third section finally in place, it was discovered that the lance had somehow twisted so that it headed away from the *Squalus* and the whole thing had to be brought up. "Excuse my English," one diver muttered to Momsen, "but those goddamn ganomes are having a field day."

By June 7th, however, the lance was down twelve feet. Diver after diver kept at it, steadily progressing, sometimes as much as four feet, other times as little as six inches. Then on June 10th the lance, having circled under the keel of the *Squalus* and on the way up her portside with perhaps eight feet to go, perversely refused to budge another inch.

A wire like a plumber's "snake" was run through the lance to finish the job. But after reaching a point believed to be about four feet beyond the nozzle it, too, would go no farther. Now a last-ditch effort was made to wash out the bottom where the snake was thought to be tantalizingly within reach. The result was harrowing.

As had happened so often, the supply of helium and oxygen in the temporary setup Momsen had rigged was exhausted. So Gunner's Mate Third Class Orval Payne from the *Falcon,* making his first dive, went down on air. On the bottom, he suddenly said that he couldn't see anything. A moment later, yelling incoherently that his lines were fouled, he announced he was going to cut himself free. Then he passed out. That saved his life. When Payne was hoisted up, knife slashes were found on his air hose.

In the afternoon a fresh consignment of the helium mix arrived from Portsmouth, and Walter Squire, the powerfully built Chief Torpedoman who had descended in the dark to sever the jammed down-haul cable of the rescue chamber, was lowered to take another crack at washing out the snake. Squire landed on the afterdeck of the *Squalus,* dragged the hose over the portside and got the water pressure he asked for, 300 pounds per square inch supplied by the *Falcon*'s fire pump. He reported gouging a hole some two feet wide and four feet deep where he thought the tip of the snake might be, and then said that he was starting a second one. But he had been laboring without letup for nearly fourteen minutes and Momsen would have none of it.

"Okay," Squire reluctantly replied, "ready to come up." But despite repeated calls, that was the last word from him. "Haul him up," Momsen ordered. The tenders handling his lines noted that Squire seemed exceptionally heavy. Befuddled by his tremendous exertion, he had opened the pressure valve on his suit. At 150 feet, he "blew up" and shot uncontrollably to the surface alongside the *Falcon,* floating helplessly in his distended suit like a grotesque parody of the balloon figures featured in Macy's annual Thanksgiving Day parade.

Without hesitation master diver James McDonald jumped overboard, splashed his way to Squire's side, wrestled him onto the diving stage which had been brought up at the first sign of danger and closed the valve. It was an amazing performance—McDonald could not swim. "I just didn't think about it," he said afterward.

On the *Falcon* with his helmet off, Squire was out cold, his face blue. His limp body, suit and all, was rushed into the decompression chamber where Dr. Willmon and Chief Pharmacist's Mate Harold David accompanied him on a wild ride into higher pressure. When the needle on the chamber gauge registered seventy-five pounds, Squire showed signs of coming to. As he did, his eyes still glazed, he began to thrash around furiously, crying out in terrible pain.

It was all Willmon and David could do to hold him down. So Momsen sent in his top bends expert, Lieutenant O. D. Yarbrough, and for added muscle diver McDonald. After a four-minute wait in the outer lock to equalize the pressure, they were ready to assist Willmon and David. The four of them cut away Squire's suit. In about half an hour, he had calmed down, although he remained in great pain and rambled on crazily. Cradling his head, Yarbrough now attempted to reach the stricken diver by leading him back through his ascent. "Squire," he kept repeating, "you are standing by to come up. Can you hear me? You are ready to come up."

Finally Yarbrough got through. "I am standing by to come up," Squire said. Then, suddenly, his eyes rolled back, he let go an anguished scream, grabbed the chamber's telephone cable and, in a pathetic effort to climb it, tore it off the wall. Then he lapsed into unconsciousness again.

Yarbrough patiently went through the same procedure, advancing his simulated ascent somewhat. "Squire," he said over and over, "you are coming up." Next, matching his words with a slow drop in pressure, he told him, "Squire, you are on the stage . . . you are on the stage."

Squire moaned fitfully. With a deep sigh, he at last answered, "I'm on the stage." Duplicating exactly the sequence of a normal ascent in the sea, continually reducing the pressure in the chamber, interrupted by brief flurries of panic, Yarbrough brought him all the way up. Finally at 8 P.M. on June 10th, after three and a half hours, Squire seemed to have recovered completely and was taken out of decompression.

Eleven minutes later, however, he developed an agonizing pain in his left arm and was promptly returned to the chamber. Although the bends had struck once more, this time Squire's mind was clear. The pain subsided under twenty-five pounds of pressure which was gradually lowered during what the divers called an overnight "soak."

When he was removed in the morning, Momsen handed him a three-day pass. "Stay drunk until your money runs out," he advised. Then, at a conference of the salvage staff, he managed to observe with a dry nicety that diving was not without its dangers. Nobody argued.

On June 15th, the original lance was abandoned. Every attempt to find the elusive snake had failed. "Come on, now," Momsen needled his dispirited divers, "think of all the lessons we've learned."

He was, in fact, far from downhearted. A new lance he and McKee had devised was being brought in from Portsmouth that morning. It featured improved couplings so the pipe sections would not slip out of alignment, as well as holes dotting its sides to keep the mud washed out, especially when the nozzle was headed up.

Best of all, the bugs in the helium hat had been ironed out and dives on air could at last be eliminated. The basic problem was that the synthetic mix had been clogging up in the helmet's internal circulating system by a combination of freezing in such low water temperature and too rapid expansion of gas as it passed through a tiny suction tube. Under the direction of Dr. Behnke the canister of soda lime used to sop up excess carbon dioxide was replaced by one containing a caustic potash compound, Shell Natron. Equally efficient as a CO_2 absorbent, it also had an enormous appetite for moisture which made it a perfect dehumidifier. The tube, meanwhile, had undergone several design revisions to get a proper gas flow at the depth the *Squalus* was in.

A new telephone setup developed by the Radio Corporation of America also made a huge difference. Phone communications had been so erratic that divers were often forced to shut off their air supply momentarily to hear a message from the surface, which in turn caused a faster CO_2 build-up. But the noise of the recirculating helium was so much greater than open ventilation that Momsen called on an old friend, Harvard's Dr. Philip Drinker, for help. Drinker quickly produced a tiny muffler along the lines of those in automobile exhaust pipes. It worked so well that Boatswain's Mate Second Class George Crocker, using it for the first time, asked to be hauled up after descending ninety-five feet; unnerved by the silence, he was sure he wasn't getting enough gas.

Not every dive from then on was hitchless. There were simply too many factors that could go wrong. But with few exceptions, the helium hat had a magical effect on morale and work capacity. Some of the men found the electrically heated underwear, controlled by a storage battery on the *Falcon,* bulky to move around in. But it was a necessary evil. When a couple of divers requested permission to go down without it, Momsen decided to let them find out for themselves. They were barely on the bottom before they were pleading to come up.

As it was, besides the big helium hat, a diver was encased in a heavy rubberized canvas suit. Cemented to his sleeves were mitten-like gloves split into two-finger partitions. Around his waist he had a belt loaded with lead, supported by cross straps and held down by a third strap running under his crotch. Finally, his legs tightly laced to prevent them from filling with gas and upsetting his buoyancy distribution, he wore rubber shoes with thick lead soles for additional weight and stability. Altogether it amounted to more than two hundred pounds of gear.

Work with the new lance was started as soon as it arrived—on June 15th. In an operation as delicate as this, Momsen had constantly been on the alert for any bickering or temper tantrums among his men. Now he had to struggle to restrain his own anger. Instead of the six-foot lengths of piping he had specified, they were an awkward eight feet long. Even with the helium hat, it made everything that much more difficult.

After the nozzle and sixteen feet of the lance had been shoved into the mud and clay, it took three dives to connect the next section. Then things picked up. Standing on the deck of the *Squalus,* divers alternately attached new sections of pipe, guided the hose into position and pushed down as hard as they could while water from the *Falcon*'s pump roared through it.

On the afternoon of June 20th, after the previous day's progress had been measured in inches, Martin Sibitsky excitedly reported that his section had gone through "with a run." An expectant hush settled over the *Falcon.* With more than forty feet of the lance circling the *Squalus,* it was just a matter of time now. Rather than fiddling with another section, Momsen lowered Ship's Fitter Second Class Virgil Aldrich to see if he could work a wire through the lance. Then the *Falcon* erupted in cheers. Aldrich had rammed it some sixty feet. Somewhere on the other side of the *Squalus* it was sticking out of the bottom. At 5 P.M. diver Osco Havens dropped down to find it. But, at that hour in the murky gloom, after trying for twelve minutes he had to give up.

The next day, leaving "Joe Boats" Morrison in charge of the divers, Momsen went ashore for the first time since salvage operations had been launched. It was his forty-fourth birthday. As it happened, it was also Admiral Cole's sixty-fourth. The two men were celebrating over cocktails when word reached them that the wire had been located at last. "Well, Swede," Cole inquired, "what do you think?"

"Admiral," Momsen solemnly replied, "I think this is just about the best Martini I've ever tasted."

Once the end of the wire that had been pushed through the lance had been tied to a line running back up to the *Falcon*, progressively larger cables were passed through the lance. Then the lance itself was pulled all the way around the submarine and raised to the surface.

By June 29th, despite some nasty weather, hoses had been attached to all the submarine's ballast tanks and 360 tons of diesel oil had been taken out of her fuel tanks. There had also been one of those near misses below that made Momsen's flesh crawl. Ship's Fitter Second Class Edward Jodrey was sliding routinely along the descending line when the *Falcon* rolled violently in an unexpected swell. The line first went slack and then snapped back, sending Jodrey flying off it. All that saved him from the squeeze was the tight rein on his lifeline that Momsen had ordered maintained for every diver after Thompson's fall.

The unpredictable sea had the whole salvage staff jumpy. More than thirty different hoses, ropes and cables were draped over the *Falcon*'s side. The possibility of all this "spaghetti," as the divers called it, tangling or breaking loose was a constant nightmare. And one bad storm could do it. But the crisis, when it came, caught everyone off guard.

The tug *Sagamore,* on July 3rd, arrived from Postsmouth with a barge loaded with salvage equipment. She hove to seemingly well clear of the *Falcon.* Suddenly a stiff wind sprang up and her anchor began dragging the bottom. Moments later she had fouled the *Falcon*'s windward mooring. The *Sagamore*'s skipper desperately tried to steam free, but her churning propeller sliced right through it.

As the *Falcon* now swung inexorably leeward, officers and men alike scrambled frantically along her deck to slacken everything leading to the *Squalus,* weeks of backbreaking labor in the balance, while a small boat dashed out to lay a new mooring. By nightfall the *Falcon* had been hauled back into position. As a result of incredible individual effort, every line and hose was still intact, either having been played out or buoyed off—with one harrowing exception.

The precious main cable under the stern of the Squalus had started to strand before anyone could get to it. Whether it had parted or not nobody knew. In the dark a diver was sent down to find out. Feeling his way along the cable, he discovered at ninety-eight feet that it had not been completely severed. He was able to apply a clamp below the stranded section and the cable was finally made fast to the *Falcon.* It had been a day of dreadful tension. But the thought in everybody's mind was that now perhaps the worst was over. As Lieutenant Karl Wheland, one of Momsen's assistant diving officers, wearily observed, "What else can go wrong?"

The basic plan to lift the *Squalus* off the ocean floor, as conceived by Construction Corps officers, involved several closely coordinated moves. To give her as much buoyancy as possible, compressed air would be blasted into the ballast tanks girdling her hull to blow out all the water in them. More air would be pumped into her fuel tanks. But the main lifting power would come from a number of pontoons straddling the submarine fore and aft.

These pontoons were actually big steel cylinders, thirty-two feet long and thirteen feet in diameter. Once they were flooded, they would be lowered into the sea and hooked up to the chain and cable slings that had been put around the *Squalus*. Then the water would be blown out of them, giving each pontoon a total lift capacity of eighty tons as it headed back toward the surface.

While they operated on a fairly simple principle, in practice they were fantastically unwieldy monsters to handle. Momsen, of all the officers on hand, was the only one who had any real working experience with them. They had been originally appropriated in 1929 by Congress after the *S-4* tragedy and he had taken two of them with him on his tour of submarine commands to demonstrate the lung and the rescue chamber.

He and his divers began placing them on July 4th. Midway through the tortuous job, Momsen had a sentimental reunion with an old friend, Commander Henry Hartley, who arrived to replace Commander McCann as a technical aide on Cole's staff. Hartley had commanded the *Falcon* when she helplessly stood by both the *S-51* and the *S-4*. As they talked of those days over a mug of coffee, Hartley said, "By God, Swede, you ought to be feeling pretty proud of yourself." It was not an idle comment. Besides the *Thetis,* since the rescue of the *Squalus* crew, the world had been rocked by another great underseas catastrophe. The French submarine *Phenix* on a training cruise had gone down off Indochina, all seventy-one men aboard her lost.*

Finally, on July 12th, despite some edgy moments in a can-

* The circumstances surrounding the fate of the *Phenix* were never known. She sank in about 300 feet of water on June 16, 1939. Just a few days earlier, because of the rescue chamber's performance in bringing up the *Squalus* survivors, the French Navy had placed an order for four of them.

tankerous sea, the seven pontoons to be used in this first lift
attempt were set at varying depths above the *Squalus*. Five were
over her flooded after compartments. The upper two of these,
positioned side by side at a depth of eighty feet, were called
"control" pontoons, because when they reached the surface they
would check the rising stern of the submarine at that point. Over
the bow there were just two pontoons—one at 140 feet and a
single control pontoon at ninety feet.

With all the hoses to the ballast tanks, fuel tanks and pontoons
connected to a central complex on the *Falcon* which would regulate
the flow of compressed air into them, the plan was to bring up the
stern, then the bow. Once the *Squalus* was off the ocean floor, since
she was headed away from Portsmouth, the tug *Wandank* would
tow her stern-first underwater in a northwesterly direction along a
course previously sounded by the *Sculpin*. To keep the chain and
cable slings holding the forward pontoons from slipping off the
stricken submarine during the lift, they had been carefully rigged
behind her still-extended bow diving planes. As for those holding
the after pontoons, Momsen could only hope that they had been
successfully guided between the keel of the *Squalus* and her
propeller struts. "Anyway," he told "Joe Boats" Morrison, "we'll
know soon enough."

The "blow and tow," as it was named, would begin the next
morning, July 13th, if the weather was favorable. And it was—the
sky clear and the North Atlantic, for once, glassy calm. With the
diving phase of the operation now completed, the salvage officer,
Lieutenant Commander Floyd Tusler of the Construction Corps,
was in command of the lift. Momsen and Morrison, meanwhile,
would each take out a motor whaleboat manned by divers to board
the control pontoons when they surfaced.

On the *Falcon,* as Tusler directed blasts of air through his
multiple hoses, there were no more interested spectators than

Oliver Naquin and thirteen of the *Squalus* survivors who had been assigned to duty with the overworked salvage crew. In measured succession, the blowing continued.

Around Momsen's whaleboat the bubbling was slow at first. Minute by minute it gradually built up, the bubbles getting bigger and bigger, no longer coming up one or two at a time but bursting out of the sea in mountainous piles, then tumbling down wildly into the green water, spreading out over it in a widening white maelstrom, boiling furiously now, vomiting forth masses of giant jellyfish, underneath it all the thunderous crescendo of an ocean gone mad. Momsen, as he hovered around its edge, had never seen or heard anything like it before.

Suddenly, in the middle of this raging caldron, the two control pontoons over the after compartments roared into view right on schedule. For a moment it seemed as if they had broken loose from their restraining cables. But then they settled back into the water —and held. Momsen and Morrison headed for them in their whaleboats, secured their flood valves and prepared them for towing. The initial phase of the lift had been completed. The stern of the *Squalus* was some eighty feet off the bottom.

Shortly after 4 P.M. that day the pontoons over the bow were blown, followed by main ballast tank No. 1 just below the forward torpedo room. When this didn't produce enough lift, air was blasted into the larger No. 2 ballast tank immediately aft. But as this was being done, before all the water could be cleared out of it, the bow began to rise. In the midst of another volcanic eruption of the sea, Momsen saw the forward control pontoon shoot to the surface. He instantly raced toward it. As he did, however, the lower pontoon, set at 140 feet, also surged up. Instinctively he knew something had gone badly wrong—and he was right. The momentum of the bow sweeping up, the expanding air in the No. 2 ballast tank emptying it even more as it rose, all the free water within the *Squalus* now surging aft, had let loose hundreds of tons of converging forces beyond restraint.

Then, pontoons slamming together, air rushing out of broken hoses, snapped cables whipping around him as he ordered the whaleboat put in reverse, it happened. Twenty feet in front of Momsen, the snout of the *Squalus* leaped out of the sea like some great wounded shark, towering over him and his men. She came almost straight up. While he gazed up in awe, she climbed perhaps thirty feet and hung there for a fraction of a second—the sight of the water streaming over the small "192" on her bow etched forever in his mind—before disappearing with a sibilant whoosh.

After forty-nine days of trying to salvage her, the *Squalus* was back on the bottom.

11

NOT EVEN THE STILTED LANGUAGE OF HIS REPORT TO THE CHIEF of Naval Operations could conceal Admiral Cole's chagrin: "With the advantage of knowledge gained by experience, it is now possible to conjecture that the unfortunate results of the lift might have been avoided if certain precautions had been taken, such as the use of two pontoons at the upper level forward for control instead of one."

The divers were especially bitter. Their endless descents day after day, each heightening the odds that one of them might not return, the staggering task of readying the *Squalus* for the lift—all reduced to a bad joke in a matter of minutes by what they felt was an incredible miscalculation by the Construction Corps people in letting their quarry slip away just when she was within reach. As they stood clustered in downcast little groups, a near gale-force wind out of the south that sent the *Falcon* lurching drunkenly underfoot did nothing to improve their spirits the next day.

Privately Momsen was as critical. He thought that after the

smaller No. 1 ballast tank proved unequal to the job of providing the bow with sufficient buoyancy, it should have been reflooded before trying to blow the big No. 2 tank. "Hell," he told Morrison, "you can't control a half-blown ballast tank coming up."

Still, they had to go on and he had no intention of allowing any post-mortem grousing among the divers to get out of hand. This time the ganomes wouldn't do. Addressing them, he laid it on the line: "All right, our little house of cards has fallen down. In case any of you are wondering what we're going to do, I'll let you in on a secret. We're going to build a better one."

Despite his soft-spoken voice, the impassive demeanor that masked so much anxiety whenever a diver went down, his seemingly easy ways, there was always about Momsen an aura of steely authority. When he fixed you with his eyes, you knew you were in a presence; even in the most intimate circumstances, none of his men would ever dream of calling him anything except "Mr. Momsen." But now, as he finished talking to them, a diver among those gathered around him shouted, "You tell 'em, Swede!"

Just sorting out the lines and hoses in the cramped deck space of the *Falcon* was enough of a chore. Then, two days after the *Squalus* had gone berserk, the sea subsided to a point where the four pontoons that had surfaced could be boarded and made ready for towing back to Portsmouth and a complete overhaul. This left three pontoons, their condition and whereabouts still to be determined, and the biggest mystery of all—the *Squalus* herself.

Obviously, when a diver could get to her, she would be an unholy mess, wrapped in hundreds of feet of twisted cables, chains and hawsers. But was she buried even deeper than before? How had she landed—keel down so that divers could utilize her deck, or was she on her side, making their work more treacherous than ever? Finally, was she flooded throughout now, the forward compartment hatches forced open because of the drastic change in pressure? On the morning of July 16th a friend sent him a clipping from the Boston *Post* which said that the "ill-starred submarine may be a total loss." After scanning it, Momsen remarked, "He must be trying to cheer me up."

That afternoon the first diver, Adrian Vanderheyden, went down with a manila line to locate the pontoons. He got to about ninety feet before he ran into a snarl of hoses and had to spend the rest of his stay underwater clearing as much of it as he could. The next man didn't fare any better. But the third diver, on the day's last descent, managed to locate two pontoons still fastened to their slings around the submarine's stern.

This was tremendously encouraging news. Despite the lunging, careening course the *Squalus* had taken, it meant that the appalling prospect of attempting to pass a new lance through the mud and clay could be forgotten. As for the third pontoon, set originally at 200 feet, no trace of it was to be seen.

For the moment Momsen abandoned the search for it. Instead he would concentrate on the two pontoons he knew about. Even so, getting them into shape was no cinch. It took fourteen dives, miraculously without an accident, to clear the bewildering web of fouled cables around them, painstakingly replace broken air hoses and open blow and flood valves.

Next Ship's Fitter First Class Harry Frye descended to inspect the afterdeck of the *Squalus*. Almost at once he lost his bearings, and his matter-of-fact report to a yeoman, which Momsen required of every diver when he came up, gave them a grim picture of what they could expect. "On landing on the submarine," Frye said, "I got fouled up in loose ends of wires. I could not move around to distinguish what side I was on, port or starboard. I thought the descending line was supposed to be on starboard side. Made report 'approximately six-degree list to starboard' but discovered later that descending line was on the portside."

Lieutenant Morrison confirmed the port list at six degrees.

The *Squalus* had started to roll as she slid back into the sea; luckily it had not fully developed before she hit down again. While noting a fantastic maze of hoses and lines, Morrison was also able to pick his way gingerly through them to make another welcome find. The forward torpedo hatch was still secure.

Momsen decided to work around the snake-like tangle swaddling the submarine as much as possible. The exertion of a "general house cleaning" at that depth was simply too demanding. Subsequent dives brought more good news. While the bow pontoon sling was irretrievably lost, the bow planes which held it in place had somehow escaped being sheared off, the stern was not buried in the muck as deeply as it had been and the three forward compartments seemed to be free of water.

It was, nonetheless, suicidal going for the divers. They had to check each coupling and salvage valve on the *Squalus,* change every hose that had been damaged, get a new chain under the bow, bring up the two pontoons that had been found, and chase down and at last pinpoint the missing pontoon where it rested nearly upright on the ocean floor; just raising it required six days.

As if this were not enough, a round of head colds raced through the closely quartered divers, knocking a number of them off the duty roster; the congestion in their Eustachian tubes made it impossible for them to adjust their ears to pressure changes. Then a three-day blow out of the northeast sent huge swells to batter them. After it had passed, a dense fog bank rolled in—and seemed to sit on them forever. It brought everything to a standstill. Even on a clear day, visibility below was a maddening, unpredictable affair, one minute as much as fifty feet and an hour later in the shifting currents less than the length of a diver's arm.

Nothing depressed Momsen more than the mist-laden shroud that enveloped them. Standing in it with Morrison, the *Falcon* strangely hushed, the sound of the sea more sensed than heard, the silence broken only by monotonous blasts across the water from Coast Guard picket boats to warn off passing ships, he finally exploded. "Jesus," he said, "how I hate it."

"What's that, sir?"

"Fog! There's not a damn thing you can do about it."

Yet with it all, by August 3rd the last pontoon was on its way back to Portsmouth for repairs. August 3rd was a red-letter day for another reason. It marked the official promotion of Lieutenant Commander Momsen. While he had said nothing about it, word leaked out and on the *Falcon*'s fantail he was surrounded by grinning divers who presented him with the gleaming scrambled-egged hat of a Navy commander. "Well," he said after recovering his aplomb, "that's a mighty fine-looking hat. I hope it fits."

"Commander," Cole said quietly, "I have no doubt it will."

The pontoon arrangement for the second try at lifting the *Squalus* would be considerably different. Instead of the five pontoons over the stern used in the first lift, there would be six. Three control pontoons were to be placed at eighty feet, an intermediate pontoon at 160 feet and the lowest two at 200 feet.

More drastic changes were in store for the bow. There would be one pontoon 200 feet down and this time three control pontoons seventy-five feet below the surface to prevent a repeat of the performance of July 13th.

Despite a series of line squalls that sent winds raging, however briefly, up to sixty knots, the pontoons were ready for the second lift early on the morning of August 12th. Other than their new arrangement, everything else remained essentially the same. Since the *Squalus* was still headed away from Portsmouth, she would be towed stern-first by the *Wandank* on a northwesterly course for about a mile and a half until she grounded, according to the *Sculpin*'s soundings, in 170 feet of water. Then, if sufficient buoyancy could be maintained, the tow would be promptly resumed northward to a hard sand bottom, around ninety feet deep, between the Isles of Shoals and the mainland, to prepare for a final run up the Piscataqua.

Lieutenant Commander Tusler would again direct the blowing of the ballast tanks, fuel tanks and pontoons from the *Falcon.* Momsen and Morrison were to embark once more in whaleboats to secure the pontoons, follow along to keep their lines from fouling and give them an "occasional pat for good luck."

At 6:30 A.M. the initial phase of the lift began in earnest. Again over the submarine's stern, Momsen watched the steady build-up of bubbles and heard the awesome rumbling beneath him that culminated three hours later in an explosion of white water. In the middle of it the three after control pontoons bounced up, disappeared momentarily and came slowly back into view lined up "like soldiers on parade." Divers boarded them immediately, precariously balancing themselves on their rounded tossing topsides, and by eleven o'clock Momsen signaled that they had been secured.

Then a tense expectancy settled over the little fleet as work on the bow started. Since the control pontoons had been blown during the night, there was much less surface boiling now as compressed air was sent into just the lower pontoon and one fuel tank. That was all it took. Almost as if in mockery of what had occurred a month before, shortly after noon the three forward control pontoons rose gracefully to the surface. The bow of the *Squalus* was some seventy feet off the bottom, her stern down a bit more.

The *Falcon* moved back alongside the tug *Sagamore,* took aboard the cable leading to the bow of the *Squalus* and at precisely 1 P.M. on August 12th the epic job of bringing her home at last got under way. The *Wandank* started the tow at one knot, but when a strong westward tidal current developed, she increased her speed to nearly two knots and her heading slightly more to the east.

It could not be going better, Momsen thought, as he directed his whaleboat around the control pontoons. Not a thing was wrong with them. Even a southerly breeze sprang up as if to urge them on.

They were twelve minutes into the second hour of the tow, the grounding area the *Sculpin* had staked out about 800 yards in front of them, when the *Wandank*'s whistle suddenly shrieked a warning blast. The *Squalus* had stopped moving. It happened so quickly that Lieutenant George Sharp, the *Falcon*'s skipper, barely managed to avoid overrunning the tow and smashing into the precious pontoons.

There was a moment of total confusion. Then when the bow of the *Squalus* began to swing around in an arc of almost a hundred degrees, it became evident, as Momsen's divers later confirmed, that her stern had nudged into a tiny hummock rising off the ocean floor which the *Sculpin* had not noticed. It was so small that a few yards either way and it would have been missed; most of the submarine's length remained more than twenty feet above the bottom. Since it had occurred at low water, Cole was hopeful that they might free her during high tide that evening. But even after the *Wandank* increased her revolutions to eight knots, the *Squalus* refused to budge.

The idea now was to drop the upper pontoons a hundred feet to carry the *Squalus* to her next target zone five miles distant. But a whitecapped chop eliminated diving the following day and also prevented something everyone had been looking forward to—a visit to the *Falcon* by President Roosevelt, who was passing by aboard the cruiser *Tuscaloosa* to his Campobello vacation retreat in Maine.

Finally, on August 17th, after days of repositioning and checking to see that the pontoons were in balance, the complex blowing procedure for the lift was repeated, all the ballast and fuel tanks in the *Squalus* having been reflooded while the work went on. At 2 P.M. the after pontoons surged up again. In his motor whaleboat

Swede Momsen routinely waited for the bow control pontoons to appear. They didn't. "Holy smokes," he heard master diver Mc-Donald whisper behind him, "they're not coming up!"

It was exactly the same situation they had faced on July 13th. After the No. 1 ballast tank had been cleared of water, nothing happened. But the lesson had been learned. Before Lieutenant Commander Tusler started to blow the big No. 2 tank, the No. 1 tank was refilled. It worked. At 5:10 P.M. the bow lifted and the control pontoons surfaced.

Just to be on the safe side, eight-inch hawsers had been attached to supplement both the towing and restraining lines in case either had weakened in all the commotion. It was a prudent move. No sooner had the tow begun than the original restraining cable snapped.

The route the *Squalus* would be taken along was full of zigs and zags to avoid shoal water. The hazy late afternoon light only made matters worse, and this time, sounding continually, the *Sculpin* led the way. Three ships were also stationed at key points along the course. One was the submarine *Sargo;* another the Coast Guard patrol boat *410.* The third was a strange apparition out of the past, the gunboat *Sacramento,* a pre-World War I relic, last of the Navy's coal-burning vessels, in Asiatic service for so long that she had become known as "the Galloping Ghost of the China Coast," on her final mission now, replete with Chinese junk sails fore and aft, as a sort of floating hotel for the divers and salvage staff.

Hurrying against the gathering darkness, the *Wandank* cranked up to eight knots on the straight legs, slowing to one or two on the turns, without a single mishap. At 9:20 P.M. the *Squalus* slid to a gentle halt on a sandy floor ninety-two feet down, precisely as planned.

The sand was so hard-packed that divers could walk easily on it and under the submarine's bow and stern without fear. For the first time they were sent down in pairs, checking every deck hatch and making sure that all hull valves were tight. Senior members of the salvage staff couldn't resist the idea that by clearing the four flooded after compartments, there would be no need at all for the unwieldy pontoons. To do it the main engine air-induction valve had to be shut manually from the outside, something impossible at previous depths the *Squalus* had been in; but then other leaks developed, particularly around the after torpedo tubes, that nothing could be done about. And while a combination of blowing and pumping finally removed some water, the compartments remained far from empty.

Like it or not, they were back to pontoons. The Construction Corps officers on the salvage staff concluded that with the thirty-three hoses the divers had connected to the ballast tanks and fuel tanks in the *Squalus,* just two pontoons on each side of her stern would suffice. Gunner's Mate First Class Walter Harmon, who had been one of the operators in the first momentous descent of the rescue chamber, and another diver were assigned to pass cables through the propeller struts under the stern. Momsen could not help thinking how much things had changed; in fourteen minutes they accomplished what had once taken a month.

But he was a bit premature in one respect. The *Squalus* would now be towed by her bow, which was to be raised first. As the final blowing got under way, before his horrified eyes the whole forward part of the submarine lunged out of the sea, rolled heavily to port at an angle of at least sixty degrees and, with the air spilling out of her tanks, sank again. A decision was made to lift the stern anyway, but the bow would not respond and the stern was dropped back down. Chief Metalsmith James McDonald, in Momsen's whaleboat, summed up all their feelings: "We've seen the bow and now we've seen the stern. How about seeing both of them together?"

"Amen," Momsen replied.

Obviously, for complete control, two more pontoons would have to be rigged to the bow. First, however, Momsen had to find out how lopsided the *Squalus* was after her violent roll. The instrument he devised for diver Joseph Alicki lacked certain scientific refinements, but it would do. It consisted of two boards nailed at a right angle with a weighted line hanging from the top of one of them. Alicki was to set the bottom board exactly athwart the main deck and mark the point where the line touched it. Measuring the triangle formed by the mark, he calculated the submarine's port list at a still manageable thirty-four degrees.

Early on August 30th, ominously ahead of schedule, the first of the monstrous storms that start lashing the Maine coast each September swept down on them with such ferocity that the *Falcon* had to buoy off all her hoses and scurry for shelter in Portsmouth.

On September 1st she was able to return to her station. Everyone was so obsessed by the thought of finally bringing the *Squalus* in, after having lived like cloistered monks oblivious to the outside world for months, that a bulletin which would affect so many of them, posted on the *Falcon* and addressed to all naval ships and installations, hardly caused a ripple. "Germany," it read, "has entered Poland. Fighting and bombing in progress. You will govern yourselves accordingly."

The swells were still too heavy to rig the bow pontoons. A diver went down, however, to inspect the condition of the submarine and discovered that the after torpedo-room hatch had sprung open. This gave the technical aides on Cole's staff a chance to revive a pet plan Momsen had fought from the first—actual entry into the submarine. Since the hatch was open anyway, why not send a diver in to close the door to the after engine room? Most of the air used in the earlier attempt to unwater the flooded compartments had escaped through the torpedo tubes. With the door shut and the ventilation valves turned down as well, it would give them a reasonable stab at least at clearing both engine rooms and the after battery. After all, the *Squalus* was just ninety-two feet down now, not 243 feet.

Momsen was aghast. "Admiral," he said, "I don't care what depth she is in. I'd also like to point out that ninety-two feet isn't exactly like getting into a bathtub. Putting a diver in that compartment is the most dangerous thing I can think of. The diameter of the hatch is only twenty-five inches. When I was diving, I once barely squeezed through a twenty-eight-inch hatch with no room whatever to spare. And even if a man gets in there, God knows what he will encounter. Suppose his lifeline fouls, or his air hose? In my opinion, the whole idea is not only dangerous, it's unnecessary."

But he was overruled.

Momsen could not go down himself; the age limit for Navy divers was forty. And under no circumstances would he order a man to do it. His dilemma was resolved when Lieutenant Morrison volunteered to climb into the after torpedo room while Boatswain's Mate First Class Forrest Smith tended his lines on the deck outside. Before the helmet was placed over the young Lieutenant's head, Momsen approached him. "Joe Boats, take care," he said.

Then he tensely followed his progress over the phone. After landing on the *Squalus,* Morrison immediately ran into trouble. Simply trying to worm his bulky suit into the hatch trunk, as Momsen had feared, was difficult enough. That done, however, Morrison's belt and air-control valve kept catching on the rungs of the trunk ladder. In order to continue, slowly moving step by step down the ladder, he had to press his arms and hands flat against his sides. Suddenly he reported, "I've lost my air. The valve must have rubbed against something."

For what were the "longest seconds of my life," Momsen
waited. He would order Morrison hauled up only as a last resort;
jammed as he was in the narrow trunk, it would almost certainly
rupture his suit. Finally, just as he was about to risk it, Morrison
managed to work his hand up to open the valve and said, "I am
okay. I am going down. My helmet must be about two feet below
the hatch top now. Wait a minute! My shoes keep hitting something across the bottom of the trunk. I can't see what it is."

That, for Momsen, was the last straw. "Joe Boats," he ordered,
"come up."

Laboriously now, Morrison made his way back up the hatch,
aided by Smith. When he was on the submarine's deck again, they
lowered a diving lamp into the hatch. The visibility was very poor,
the water in the compartment full of silt. But they could faintly see
what the obstruction was—the face and arm of a body lying across
the bottom edge of the trunk. There seemed to be another body
just below it.

That evening Momsen requested a private audience with Admiral Cole. "Sir," he began, "if I am to remain diving officer, I
must—"

It was as far as he got. Cole cut him short. "Swede," he said, "I
know. There will be no more efforts to enter the submarine until
she is in dry dock."

A few days later Morrison was relieved from salvage duty as an
assistant diving officer to assume his first submarine command, the
Sea Lion, a transfer that had been postponed on several occasions
during the summer. "Joe Boats," Momsen told him as he prepared
to depart, "you're an outstanding officer, one of the best, and I
think you have a hell of a future ahead of you. I regret you won't
be around to see the grand finale."

"Well, sir, I don't have to say what a pleasure it's been serving
under you. I've learned a lot and I'm sorry, too, that I won't be

here. But to tell you the truth, I've seen enough to last me a long time."

Within six months Momsen would be horrified to learn of Morrison's death. He accidentally shot himself while cleaning a rifle.

On September 11th everything was set for the last lift—except the weather. During the night a southeast wind, reaching a velocity of forty knots, canceled any chance of it. By late afternoon, however, the wind had shifted around to the northwest and gradually abated. The next morning Lieutenant George Mac-Kenzie, who had relieved Morrison, came up with a chilling report after an inspection dive. The wind and sea had taken their toll. The stability of the *Squalus* was at a critical point. She was listing perceptibly more to port, at least ten degrees more; MacKenzie had actually seen her move.

Time was running out—and fast. That evening Cole got the report he had been waiting for, the forecast for September 13th: "Light to gentle north and northeast winds. Partly cloudy. Unlimited visibility. Sea smooth."

So on September 13th at 5:48 A.M. the final lift began. Cole was anxious to get the *Squalus* into the Piscataqua for high slack water at 1:30 P.M. Just past eight o'clock the stern pontoons surfaced, sank out of sight and then reappeared. The hose fitting on one of them had broken and a geyser of air and water was shooting out of the broken pipe. Momsen and his whaleboat crew scrambled aboard and got an emergency valve over it just in time. Though the pontoon was still floating, it was nearly awash.

Two hours later the bow pontoons rose and with them the periscope and the top of the conning tower. "We've got her! We've got her!" somebody shouted. But it was not to be. In spite of all the air that had been pumped into her, no sooner did the

Squalus start to broach than she rolled slowly over and sank, the stern pontoons with her. Now the bow had to be reflooded to line her up on the bottom. At noon she was completely down.

They had no choice. There wasn't even time for a diver to check her over. The entire process of blowing her was repeated at once. At 12:45 P.M. there was a furious boil of bubbles over the stern, but no pontoons. Desperately the blowing went on but nothing happened. And now for the first time during all those weeks and months they were ready to admit they had been vanquished. The *Squalus* would never be raised. On the *Falcon,* in Momsen's whaleboat, throughout every ship in the salvage flotilla, one gloomy face after another showed defeat.

Perhaps that's what it took. Nobody ever stepped forward with a better explanation. Without warning the stern pontoons bobbed up at 1:25 P.M. About an hour later, the bow pontoons emerged.

As they did, it happened. Like a huge, exhausted game fish, the *Squalus* slowly rose alongside the *Falcon,* first the periscope again, the conning tower higher and higher, tilted slightly to port, the "192" on its starboard side clearly visible, the top of the pilothouse smashed in probably during her fearful leap on July 13th, her main deck just below the surface, bits of bent and mangled rigging briefly in view until she settled down.

It was fully five minutes—after Momsen and his divers had secured the pontoons, swiftly closing one more leaking hose valve—before they were certain they had her at last. "I just learned something about myself," Momsen said. "I didn't know I could hold my breath that long."

At 3:12 that afternoon the *Wandank* began her tow; Cole had missed his high slack water, and since the narrow, twisting Piscataqua was in its ebb-tide rush toward the North Atlantic, the civilian tug *Chandler* moved in to lend a hand if necessary. The faithful old *Penacook,* meanwhile, came alongside the trailing *Falcon* to buttress her power.

They paused outside the river's mouth at 6:20. Cole faced a decision that he alone had to make. The *Squalus* was drawing about thirty-nine feet of water, and with mean low tide an hour and a half away, there were two spots he would have to pass that were at least that shallow. Yet to wait for high water invited unknown perils. "All right," he said, "let's go."

On the *Falcon,* before returning with his divers to their whaleboats, a delighted Momsen told him, "Sir, if it were permissible for a commander to slap an admiral on the back, you'd be getting an awful thump right now."

The first bad point in the channel was a little south of an old lighthouse guarding the north side of Portsmouth Harbor. And there the *Squalus* touched down. But in a superb display of seamanship the *Falcon* held steady until the *Wandank* speeded up enough to drag the submarine over the hump.

As they entered the harbor itself, the colors of each ship were solemnly lowered to half mast. Thousands of people crowded both shorelines, watching silently in the fading light as the strange, almost funereal procession slowly headed upstream. Later, after the sun went down and they were no longer able to see the bare eight feet of the conning tower that had held their fascinated gaze, they still stayed, marking the progress now by the lights of the tow ships. Then, in the hush that hung over them all in the night air, there was a great gasp. The lights had stopped moving.

From the sea the Piscataqua courses inland past the Portsmouth Navy Yard in a sweeping S-shaped curve. While rounding the lower bend of the S, the *Squalus* grounded again. It was here that the second shallow area of the channel lay. Here, too, the mad rush of the river reached its greatest fury, the currents in constant, ruthless motion except for the brief minutes of absolutely still water between tidal runs. Despite the imminence of low water, it was foaming white against the conning tower, the submarine herself beginning to swerve out of line, a new disaster in the making if she stuck there.

But the Portsmouth Harbor Master, Captain Shirley Holt, who had assumed direction of the tow, daringly brought the *Squalus* hard by the eastern edge of the channel, just skirting the rockbound tip of the yard where the shoaling was minimal, the *Wandank* straining forward until it seemed that the towline must break. At that moment the *Squalus* slid through.

At 8 P.M. she was resting on the river bottom about a hundred feet from her destination, Berth 6. Momsen's whaleboat crews quickly ran lines out to the pontoons and the *Penacook* and the *Chandler* moved in to hold her against the flood tide. As the Piscataqua rose, the *Squalus* was brought in and at 9:30 she was alongside her berth. Pumping out her compartments was begun at once to prepare her for dry dock. But for all practical purposes it was over; a hundred and thirteen days after her fatal plunge on the morning of May 23rd she had returned.

After watching for a while in the glare of the floodlights as she came eerily into view, Swede Momsen could be forgiven a bit of hyperbole he entered in his diary that night. "As I stood there," he wrote, "I thought I saw a trident and a crown rise out of the water, followed by the face of Neptune, clouded in disappointment. He had been cheated of his prize."

There was, after all, more than a little truth in it.

Pumping out the *Squalus* continued through September 14th and shortly after midnight she was nearly ready to be hauled into dry dock. By then, too, five bodies had been removed from the engine rooms, placed in gray sacks and taken to the morgue at the Portsmouth Naval Hospital.

Four hours later her rusted, battered hull was completely exposed. Seventeen more bodies were in the after torpedo room that Lieutenant Morrison had attempted to enter. It was obvious that the men had met mercifully quick deaths. The sea had swept in so fast that there had been no time for anyone even to reach for a Momsen lung; all of them were still in their racks. Torpedoman Second Class Alfred Priester, the after torpedo-room talker, was found sitting upright between a locker and a torpedo tube, earphones in place, as if waiting for a message from the control room that would never come.

Seaman Second Class John Marino, the Iowa boy on board his first submarine, was taken out of the after battery near the mess area where he would have been serving the noon meal; nobody who had scrambled out of the compartment remembered seeing him there. Seaman First Class Alexander Keegan, who had stepped out of the galley just as the dive began, was in the battery washroom.

That left two men yet to be accounted for. Cutting through the metal deck plates of the after battery with acetylene torches, they found the twenty-fifth man, Electrician's Mate First Class John Batick, where he had gone down to observe how the battery group there behaved.

But the twenty-sixth man, Cook Second Class Robert Thompson, who was napping during the dive after having prepared breakfast, was never found. Momsen had an idea of what might have taken place. After the *Squalus* was down, the men huddled in the control room heard a loud inexplicable clang. It was just possible that Thompson, caught in the compartment, had instinctively climbed up to the after battery hatch and undogged it, waiting for that moment when the pressure equalized so he could open it in a desperate effort to get out of the submarine. A pocket of trapped air then might have forced the hatch open, causing it to fall back after the air had escaped. The hatch cover, in any event, was closed during most of the salvage. Momsen's divers had gotten into the habit of ringing the ship's bell on the *Squalus* whenever they could; in order to do it they had to stand on the hatch. Then after the unexpected grounding on August 12th, as diver Jesse Duncan went toward the bell, he saw to his amazement that the hatch was open. One way or another Thompson's body had gone through it.

With the *Squalus* in dry dock, the final phase of the investigation into the disaster was at hand. The official Court of Inquiry, headed by Rear Admiral William Tarrant, had already taken written statements from all survivors, then exhaustively questioned them orally, even down to asking Quartermaster First Class Francis Murphy about the news item indirectly quoting him that the *Squalus* had been in difficulty before. Murphy denied ever saying anything like it.

Now Tarrant and members of his court, accompanied by Naquin and his executive officer, Lieutenant Walter Doyle, trooped into the control room to see if they could solve the mystery of the open main engine air-induction valve. After fluid had been fed into the hydraulic system, Doyle pulled the lever that would close both it and the main air-ventilation valve. When he did, the ventilation valve clicked shut. But the main engine valve did not move. Was this, as Naquin believed, what had happened on May 23rd? They would never know. After more fluid was pumped into the hydraulic system, Doyle pulled the lever again. This time the valves closed in tandem.

The court resumed its hearings, questioning among others Momsen and Captain Richard Edwards. In the end, it reported to the Secretary of the Navy that the loss of the *Squalus* "was due to a mechanical failure in the operating gear of the engine induction valve" and that "this mechanical failure was not discovered in time, due to either an electrical failure in the valve indicator or a mistake in reading this indicator by the operating personnel." It singled out no one person for censure, certified that the submarine's officers and crew were "well-trained and efficient" and declared that "Lieutenant Naquin displayed outstanding leadership during the sinking of the U.S.S. *Squalus* and the rescue of her survivors."

But the nuances of a Navy inquiry report, like the fine print in the time-payment plan of a shady car salesman, have to be studied with care. And Oliver Naquin would never be given what he so desperately wanted—another submarine.

He had been doomed as far back as June 11th when Captain Edwards, in his capacity as Commander Submarine Squadron Two, dispatched a memo to the Commander Submarine Force that said in part: "The *Squalus* was following the practice which has become not unusual of diving with open hull valves in induction and hull ventilation lines. This practice is considered unnecessary and dangerous."

The valves Edwards was talking about were hand-operated ones inside the submarine. Practically no submarine captain at the time bothered with them because, as Momsen said, they "were so damn hard to get at, especially the one in the forward engine room," and in a brand-new boat they tended to stick.

The report to the Secretary of the Navy noted that these valves had been open. His subsequent "action" report said: "Had these hull stop valves been closed prior to submergence . . . only the pipe lines and not the compartments would have been flooded." It didn't matter that Naquin had just been unlucky. The law of the sea prevailed; the skipper took the rap. He was reassigned, served honorably throughout World War II and retired with the rank of rear admiral.

The water had swept into the *Squalus* through the main-engine air induction valve—no one quite knew why. To prevent the possibility of the lever ever being inadvertently opened, in all submarines already in service a protective shield was added to isolate the main inductions lever from other levers adjacent to it. In every submarine built thereafter the position of the lever was changed and it was given a distinctive grip. There was another key design change. Instead of having to shut the inboard valves laboriously by handwheels against an incoming rush of sea, a man had only to trip levers and the sea pressure itself automatically closed them.

What befell the *Squalus* has yet to happen to any other submarine in the U.S. Navy. Momsen, meanwhile, left for his first captaincy since the *S-1*, the 10,000-ton *Sirius* waiting for him at the Norfolk Navy Yard. He went with a commendation in his service jacket which, after recording his "exceptional coolness, judgment, specialized knowledge and responsibility" in rescuing the thirty-three survivors of the *Squalus*, went on to state:

This was a period of the greatest diving effort in the world's history. That in 640 dives, under the most severe conditions, there was not a single loss of life or a serious personal injury speaks for the eternal vigilance, professional skill, technical knowledge and rare judgment and initiative of Commander Charles Bowers Momsen.

12

THERE REMAINED ONE BITTER IRONY IN THE DRAMA YET TO BE played out—terrifying if you live in the inevitability of fate or, if you were Swede Momsen, something simply to accept and go on.

Nine months after she had been brought in, the *Squalus* was completely refurbished, once more a sleek, silent killer, and recommissioned with a new name, the *Sailfish*. Then with the *Sculpin*— the sister submarine that had found her—she went to war. One day in 1943 the *Sculpin* was forced to the surface by a Japanese destroyer and a number of her crew captured.

In December, that same year, the old *Squalus,* now the *Sailfish,* tenaciously tracked a Japanese carrier for ten hours during a raging typhoon, fired her torpedoes and saw her sink. When the carrier went down, she took with her, locked in steel cages, twenty prisoners from the *Sculpin,* their destiny sealed the moment a man on her bridge looking the wrong way spotted a smoke bomb sent up by the stricken *Squalus* four and a half years before.

The Navy did not find out about it until after the war. When Momsen, by then a rear admiral, first heard the news, he went out and had a stiff drink—by himself.

EPILOGUE

INDOMITABLE TO THE LAST, SWEDE MOMSEN DIED A HARD DEATH, from cancer, on May 25, 1967. At his own request he had retired in 1955 as a vice admiral. But before he did, he left a profound legacy—in deed and in vision—beyond the lung, the rescue chamber, new diving techniques.

The Navy which buried him with so much pomp and ceremony and which he served with such devotion and distinction never really knew quite what to make of him. Here was no obvious fanatic, no oddball specialist to be pigeonholed, but a magnificent physical specimen in a world where appearance counts, a superb line officer with a record of matchless command ability, whose fitness reports from the first were studded with comments like "outstanding" . . . "promotion richly deserved" . . . "resourceful, capable and indefatigable" . . . "courageous" . . . "exceptional personality."

Yet here was that same man, in that quiet thoughtful way of his, sending the Bureau of Ships into a tizzy for recommending as far back as 1939: "We should start *now* to build submarines that can go to a thousand feet and make twenty knots while submerged." That was heresy enough in an era when the battlewagon was still king. But here, too, was a man who even then could pick up his favorite book, *Twenty Thousand Leagues Under the Sea,* quote from Jules Verne's Captain Nemo—"There is a powerful agent, obedient, rapid, easy, which conforms to every use, and reigns supreme on board my vessel. Everything is done by means of it. It lights it, warms it, and is the soul of my mechanical apparatus"—and astonish his fellow submarine officers by calmly saying, "We'll have something like that one day."

"I suppose," he told me once, "that the kindest thing they said about me in those days was that I had the makings of a hell of a humorist. But it becomes clear very early in military life, perhaps for good reason, that the best way to get ahead is to stay with the pack. I guess during my career I steered a course a bit too much my own. But I'm not the only one. There was Billy Mitchell, who spun off into the woods, Jim Gavin, who skidded off the road a little, and, of course, many others. When an officer with initiative and imagination leaves the middle of the road, he's bound to have trouble. His superiors get set in their ways, indifferent or even hostile to new ideas. Sometimes it's just because they didn't think of them themselves. Often when I was presenting a new proposal, I was made to feel like a felon committing a crime and ended up not only having to defend the idea but myself for daring to bring it up. But it did happen—too rarely—to have someone up the line say, 'That sounds good. Let's go.' Since my time, I think the situation is much improved."

He never quit his Navy, however, until he felt at last that he had gone as far as he could within its ranks—and when his restless mind plunged past the purely military aspects of the millions of cubic miles of water covering the earth which had now become for

him as intoxicating, as meaningful, as great a challenge as outer
space. Part man of science, part prophet, there was also deep within
him the mystique of the sea, of action and of command. In 1923,
shortly after he was given his first ship, the *O-15*, he wrote a letter
that says something about this and about himself:

Suddenly there was no one to lean on. I was responsible for the lives
of twenty-seven officers and men, for their personal safety and future
progress. At the ceremony all their families were in attendance. I could
see the wives and children looking at me, wondering perhaps if I really
could be trusted with the welfare of their bread winners.

In my training I always thought that I had it, that command would
be a cinch. Now I know what it is like. Every order I give has to be
carefully weighed. After all, a submarine is all or nothing. Once under
water those steel walls are surrounded by thousands of pounds of water
and if something goes wrong there is nothing we can do about it; just
don't let it happen!

My crew watches my every expression, every emotion, and listens
intently to my every word, whether it's an order or a casual remark.
When I am at the periscope, a dozen eyes are on me and, believe me,
they can tell exactly what's happening on the surface. They share the
pride of serving on a smart ship and the shame of one that doesn't
measure up.

Even the simple maneuver of bringing a submarine alongside of a
dock is so important. If you back and fill, break lines and start shouting
like mad, your men feel the scorn ashore and there are going to be
plenty of black eyes and cracked jaws in the beer hall that night. But if
you bring her in "like a feather," you feel them bristle with pride in
themselves and in you.

Most of all, I have found what a wide gap exists between the executive officer and the captain. He has one last check; the captain has none.
But to have your own ship, to take her to sea—and under it—what an
experience that is! I wouldn't trade it for anything.

He was the same man in war as in peace. December 7, 1941,
found Swede Momsen operations officer on the staff of the Commandant for the Fourteenth Naval District at Pearl Harbor.

Shortly after seven o'clock that Sunday morning, he was awakened by the duty officer who reported that the destroyer *Ward* had attacked and sunk an unidentified submarine just outside the great base. He immediately passed this on to the chief of staff, who "wanted further information." By 7:30 Momsen was on the way to his office, having called the Commandant himself and ordered a second destroyer, the *Monahan,* to assist the *Ward.* Twenty minutes later the *Monahan,* as the first bombs started to fall, reported ramming a second submarine—another of the now-famous midgets the Japanese had hoped to sneak into the harbor. Then, while strafing machine-gun bullets whined around him, he saw the *Arizona* blow up, the *Oklahoma* roll over.

After helping to organize a new command, the Hawaiian Sea Frontier, and serving as its assistant chief of staff, Momsen returned to his beloved submarines in early 1943, a captain now, to head up Submarine Squadron Two under the Commander Submarines Pacific, his old friend Rear Admiral Charles Lockwood—the same Lockwood whose telephone call in Washington that muggy May 23rd had sent him flying off to Portsmouth.

It would lead to another hair-raising adventure for him. Lockwood had been getting report after report from skippers returning from war patrols bitterly complaining about duds from their Mark VI torpedo exploders. Even more mystifying, most of the duds occurred at what was considered the ideal firing track—broadside at a ninety-degree angle. Yet torpedo hits were consistently more successful at less desirable, slanted angles. As far as the Bureau of Ordnance was concerned, it was all an alibi for failure; there was nothing the matter with either the torpedoes or the exploders. The situation came to a climax when the submarine *Tinosa* ran into a 19,000-ton Japanese merchantman sailing alone in broad daylight. The *Tinosa* fired a salvo of four torpedoes at an almost perpendicular ninety-five-degree angle. At least two hit—and did not explode. The merchantman put on speed and turned away, but the

Tinosa just managed to catch her with two torpedoes at a wretched tangent. Both of them exploded, however, and stopped her dead in the water. Now, at his leisure, the *Tinosa's* commander, Lieutenant Commander L. R. Daspit, moved in 875 yards abeam of his target and pumped in nine more torpedoes. Not one went off. A furious Daspit saved the last torpedo he had, returned to Pearl Harbor with it and marched into Lockwood's office with the news. But when the torpedo was taken apart, no defect could be found and the exploder, when tested, fired normally.

At this point Momsen came to Lockwood with an obvious idea—except that once again nobody had thought of it. Near Pearl was the little island of Kahoolawe with sheer cliffs in fairly shallow water. "Let's take a load of torpedoes down there," Momsen said, "and keep firing them against the cliffs until we get a dud. Then we'll see why." It was a thoroughly practical suggestion, although as Lockwood later recalled, "I suspected we would find ourselves shaking hands with Saint Peter when we tried to examine a dud warhead with six hundred and eighty-five pounds of TNT."

So the submarine *Muskellunge* departed for Kahoolawe. The experiment got off to a bad start. The first torpedo she fired exploded. But the next one didn't. "Well," said Momsen, "this is what we want." Then he, along with Lockwood and some officers and men from an escort ship, the *Chalcedony,* boarded small boats in swimming trunks and goggles to look for the dud. Momsen dived in and found it in about fifty feet of clear water, "the warhead split open with big chunks of TNT lying around." A boatswain's mate from the *Chalcedony,* an expert skin diver named John Kelly, managed to shackle a cable around the torpedo's tail and it was gingerly hauled onto the submarine rescue ship *Widgeon.* There, with everyone acutely aware that it could go off at any moment, Momsen examined its innards.

On impact the firing pin on the Mark VI exploder was supposed to travel a few inches along guides and hit the priming cap which in turn would set off the TNT. In the torpedo now on the deck of the *Widgeon,* the pin had reached the caps, barely touching them, but not hard enough to trigger an explosion. So they finally had the answer. If the torpedo hit head on, the counteraction of the collision slowed the firing pin just enough to keep it from striking the cap. When it came in on a slant, however, the deceleration of a glancing blow was much less and the torpedo would explode as planned.

More tests confirmed this and Lockwood radioed all submarine captains at sea to fire their torpedoes only at sharp or oblique angles—anything except the way they had been trained to do it. In a series of its own tests at Newport, Rhode Island, the Bureau of Ordnance glumly agreed that the exploder design was faulty and promised to come up with a solution. But while the bureau was fiddling around, Momsen with the assistance of fellow officers at Pearl Harbor, where there was perhaps a greater sense of urgency, solved the problem chiefly by cutting down the firing pin, making it lighter, and as a result reducing the amount of friction as it slipped along the guides. On September 30, 1943, the *Barb* left on a war patrol with twenty torpedoes thus modified and as a relieved Lockwood put it, "All major exploder problems suddenly disappeared."*

Throughout the summer of 1943 Momsen, admittedly "chafing

* Curiously, while the two basic works on the Navy during the war, *History of United States Naval Operations in World War II* and *United States Submarine Operations in World War II,* deal with the critical problem of torpedo duds and its eventual solution, neither one mentions Momsen. The recommendation for the Legion of Merit, which he subsequently received, describes how he initiated an "experimental program to investigate the faulty performance of submarine torpedo exploders," that when one torpedo failed to explode "Captain Momsen organized a party to recover this 'dud' for examination and at great personal risk entered the water and assisted in the recovery and examination of this live torpedo" and then "personally supervised an investigation into the weakness of the exploder. . . ."

to get back to sea," had also been immersed in masterminding a form of submarine warfare new to the Pacific. The impetus had come in the spring when Washington authorized a look into "wolf pack" tactics. The name originally derived from the swarms of German U-boats that snapped at the huge Allied convoys crossing the North Atlantic to England. Up till then the Navy had not employed such tactics for two very good reasons: there had not been sufficient American submarines to go around in the vast stretches of ocean they had to cover, and Japanese convoys were nowhere near as large. Now, however, there were enough submarines, and more and more enemy convoys increasing in size— too much for a single submarine to handle—were observed moving south from Japan through the relatively narrow confines of the East China Sea.

Various schemes were worked out on a "war games board" that once served as the wardroom dance floor for the Pearl Harbor submarine command. The upshot differed radically from German techniques. U-boats in the North Atlantic, after being directed to form packs by radio from shore stations, made their assaults in a wild melee. Submarines in American packs, on the other hand, would attack in close coordination, communicating with each other via low-frequency sound waves underwater. Also the American packs would be much smaller. While Japanese convoys were getting bigger, they still rarely exceeded more than twelve ships. So the ideal number of submarines for each U.S. pack was finally fixed at three. The basic strategy called for one submarine to hit the starboard flank of a convoy, another the port flank, the third to tag along behind to finish off the cripples.

On October 1st Momsen, in recognition of his tireless planning, was given the honor of taking the first American wolf pack out of Midway into the East China Sea. Two of his three submarines, as well as one skipper, had never been in combat before. Despite this, and facing all the unexpected hazards of an experimental mission, his group returned some six weeks later with 101,000 tons of enemy shipping sunk or damaged and a lot of lessons learned. Lockwood promptly utilized them, and before the war was over, a hundred and seventeen more wolf packs sallied forth against the Japanese with enormous success. For evolving "a doctrine of attack whereby submarines could be organized into an attack group capable of operating deep in enemy-controlled waters while maintaining full striking power," Swede Momsen received the Navy Cross.

During the next six months, he wore two hats as Commander Submarine Squadron Four and Chief of Staff, Commander Training Command, Submarine Forces, U.S. Pacific Fleet. Then in May, 1944, he was ordered to Washington by the Navy's Commander in Chief himself, Admiral Ernest J. King. As he flew eastward, an excited Momsen couldn't help wondering what such an unusual summons was about. All sorts of glittering assignments in store for him danced in his head. To require his personal presence, he was sure it must be awfully important.

The crusty King got right to the point. "Swede," he barked, "you have to clean up this damn mail mess!" It has to be a joke, Momsen thought, to be relegated to some sort of postman after all he had done. But it wasn't. "I'm not kidding," King continued. "You think the biggest worry I have right now is blowing Japs out of the water—well, you're wrong! It's the Navy's mail and *my* mail." King pointed to a sack spilling over with letters in a corner of his office. "Every one of them is from a congressman or a senator and they're all on the same subject—our mail service and, specifically, how lousy it is. They're driving me crazy. Something has to be done. You have an absolutely free hand." As Momsen started to leave, King sugar-coated the pill. "Swede," he said, "do this for me and I promise you a command."

Once in the project, Momsen tackled it, as he would any problem, with painstaking research and bold answers. The fact was that he was soon enjoying himself immensely just raising hell with established procedures that nobody had ever questioned. His first act—cutting down V-mail—sent the Navy's postal service into shock. V-mail consisted of a single sheet of paper which was photographed on rolls of film, each bearing 1,600 letters, and reproduced in fleet post offices for eventual distribution. The men despised it, as Momsen said, because aside from normal censorship, it gave "every Tom, Dick and Harry" a chance to read what they had written. But this was really beside the point. The theory behind it was that it would speed a letter's delivery. In fact, he discovered, exactly the opposite was true. Sailors, Waves and civilian workers were actually wasting thousands of man-hours trying to keep track of the whole reprocessing system.

Next he went after the bonding of all mail clerks, a routine that often took months. "It doesn't make any sense in war," he said. "Let's get rid of it." Navy postal officers told him, "You'll never get away with it. The bonding companies won't stand for it and neither will Congress." But when he approached bonding executives, they practically fell on their knees at the prospect. To a man they said, "It's one of our biggest nuisances." Then he took care of Congress by getting the Navy to assume the risk after he produced statistics that showed the cost of bonding was far greater than any loss being suffered.

After that, a tour of the Pacific turned up some interesting items. First were the home-town newspapers. As many as thirty or forty goodhearted citizens would take out a subscription for one man. In Pearl Harbor alone Momsen found ten tons of home-town papers awaiting shipment. In installation after installation, he observed that as mailbags piled up in warehouses, the last ones in were the first ones out—leaving the mail on the bottom placidly in place for as much as six or eight months. In Guam he accidentally overheard a fascinating piece of intelligence. Two sailors at the airstrip were trying to bum rides, one to Honolulu, the other to San Francisco. "Okay," the dispatcher said to them. "There's a plane going out in twenty minutes. I'll throw off a couple of mailbags." To spice things up, there was also the prominent admiral flying in fresh vegetables from Australia to garnish his table and a flag officer in Alaska shipping feed by air for some cattle he had; if this meant there wasn't enough room for mail, it was simply too bad.

On his return, Momsen sat down and totally revamped the Navy's postal setup. At the end of November, 1944, he went in to see Admiral King and said, "I think I've done the job."

"Yes," King replied. "I guess you have. I must say that my mail has improved considerably. Now I have another little job for you." At that Momsen winced. But King was as good as his word. The "little job" was to captain the mighty *South Dakota,* flagship of the Pacific battle line.

With Momsen as her skipper, the *South Dakota* was in action in the Marianas, at Iwo Jima, supported the invasion of Okinawa and was the first U.S. warship to bombard the main Japanese island of Honshu. It also resulted in one of the more memorable bits of dialogue during World War II.

Cruising off Okinawa Momsen was on the bridge watching as the *South Dakota* had nearly finished taking on shells and powder from an ammunition ship running alongside. Suddenly, from one of the forward gun turrets below him, a cloud of ugly yellow smoke belched forth. There was more smoke. Then a muffled report and the great ship shuddered. Somehow the worst possible thing was happening: there had been an explosion and, with the lives of over a thousand crewmen at stake, the *South Dakota* was moments away from blowing up. Instantly Momsen called his damage control officer: "Flood all magazines, Number Two turret!" Out of the corner of his eye, he could see the ammunition ship scuttling off and, for that matter, every other ship within sight.

There was a second explosion and in quick succession three more, the *South Dakota,* despite her massive size, quivering violently with each one. At this point the battle line commander, Rear Admiral W. A. "Ching" Lee, headquartered on board and routed out of his cabin by all the tumult, reached Momsen's side on the bridge. "For Christ's sake," he exclaimed, "what's going on?"

"I think the forward magazines are exploding."

"Good God, man, what are you doing about it?"

"I've ordered the magazines flooded."

"Well, are they doing it?"

"I hope so, Admiral, but I'm not going to call them *now* to find out." Momsen pointed his finger at a spot in the sky ahead of them. "Anyway, we'll know soon enough. If they haven't, that's where we'll be in about thirty seconds."

The near disaster led to another hassle between Momsen and Naval bureaucracy. The incident that almost did in the *South Dakota* was rare—but it had occurred, inexplicably, before on other ships in similar circumstances. This time Momsen had an eyewitness who was entering the magazine at the first flash; luckily the door he was about to go through closed toward him and he was saved. According to him, it happened just as two men were carrying a drum of power into the magazine. Inside each drum, made of steel, was a silk bag which actually contained the powder. Momsen concluded that the friction between the steel and the silk had produced a spark of static electricity that set off the powder. Bureau of Ordnance experts politely responded that he was nuts. But he persisted and they finally agreed to try out his theory. Night and day for a month the simulated loading of powder continued without letup. On the last day the Bureau of Ordnance reported getting a spark. That ended the argument—and the use of silk bags for gunpowder—for good.

In November, 1945, the war over, Momsen faced the most massive test yet of his ingenuity, leadership and command ability. Win or lose, Japan had been determined to leave its stamp on Asia forever. And in the wake of Japan's conquests—in China, down the Malay Peninsula, throughout all the islands of the far Pacific —came nearly six million Japanese colonizers. Now they would all be returned to their homeland. And the man who was going to have to get them there was Momsen. It would be the largest, fastest population movement in history. To do it, he was given ninety-six Liberty ships for passengers, six more which he turned into hospital ships, and eighty-five LSTs. But this was just the beginning. Every vessel would be crewed, officers and men, by Japanese and he had to train them before repatriation could even get under way.

Since these ships were American-owned but Japanese-manned, the flag of neither nation could properly be flown. So Momsen gleefully devised his own colors—green and red divided diagonally. Despite the flag's tenuous legal standing, it soon became the most familiar sight in the western Pacific. Before he was finished, besides his Liberty ships and LSTs, he pressed into service fifty Japanese merchantmen and as many more U.S. Navy ships as he could grab at one time or another, including two carriers and two cruisers. And without a single mishap, without any outbreak of disease in boats crammed to the gunwales with people, he brought back some 5,700,000 Japanese in less than a year.

During one three-month period in this stupendous operation, the total embarkation and debarkation figures happened to coincide exactly. "Amazing, Momsen, simply amazing," General Douglas

MacArthur, his imperious superior, remarked after reading the
report. "How do you do it?"

"General," he solemnly replied, "it's really not that difficult. It's
just a matter of arranging for the same number of births as deaths
once you're at sea."

Although he would go on to other commands, Swede Momsen's
most spectacular contribution to the Navy—indeed one so revolutionary that its ramifications are still being felt and will continue
to be for years to come—began in 1948 shortly after he was
appointed to a new post, Assistant Chief of Naval Operations for
Undersea Warfare. The Navy, as it then existed, would never be
the same again. It was a time when Captain—later Rear Admiral—Hyman Rickover was working on his experimental atomic-
power plant. As a matter of cost efficiency, the plant would be tried
out first in the submarine *Nautilus*. But in a Navy firmly in the
control of aircraft-carrier admirals, the *Nautilus* was essentially a
laboratory; if it worked, the plan called for bigger nuclear plants
—for carriers and their escorts.

Momsen saw something else. Submarines, because of the limitations of battery power, were actually surface ships that occasionally
dipped below the waves. Their whole design—ironically, with a
few modifications, even the *Nautilus*—was predicated on this
principle. Yet with nuclear power the advent of a true submersible,
which would only occasionally come to the surface, was at hand.
Given the right kind of hull, as Momsen put it, "a submarine no
longer would have to slink along like a frightened cow at one or
two knots at a depth of a few hundred feet while her tormentors
rained depth charges on top of her until their supply was exhausted." Instead she could now be the aggressor, the Navy's new
capital ship, backbone of the fleet.

But how could he get such a project through? To speak openly of what he privately foresaw—submarines capable of sixty knots, able to dive to 10,000 feet, to whip anything they encountered on the surface—was to invite a fast ride to the nearest booby hatch. Fortunately that young Lieutenant who had arrived in Washington in 1929 crushed to find his scheme for a diving bell so rudely dismissed had subsequently acquired a marvelous guile to circumvent establishment thinking. He would never use it to better advantage than he did now. In a carrier-oriented Navy, funds for submarine development were at the bottom of the list, but anti-submarine-warfare techniques had high priority. It was just the opening Momsen needed. He submitted his proposal as a *target* for submarine hunter-killer groups to practice on and received an enthusiastic go-ahead.

Since she would not be armed, the whole thing would be in the hands of designers at the Bureau of Ships. Momsen's instructions to them were brief: "Forget about surface performance. Think only about submerged capability which will provide the utmost in speed with a minimum of power."

Endless tests were conducted under the direction of a special committee of Naval and civilian scientists. An investigation was made into every conceivable area—including aircraft and blimps—for clues to the streamlined hull Momsen requested. In all, twenty-five models were produced and discarded before the right one emerged. She was called the *Albacore* and she was a revelation in appearance and performance. She had a short, round, smooth, whale-like body, broken only by a slender, rakish, dorsal-fin tower rising out of her back. Since the twin screws carried on conventional submarines were merely an aid for surface maneuverability and actually decreased her thrust through water, she also had just one five-bladed propeller.

Her control room resembled an airplane cockpit, her movements regulated by a "stick," her diving and steering operators strapped into bucket seats with safety belts. The rest of her crew—as she dived, turned, stopped and started with fantastic swiftness—were forced to hang on to overhead straps like subway riders. Even in the brief bursts of speed allowed by her ordinary battery-driven motors, the *Albacore* drove antisubmarine forces crazy, ran rings around the nuclear *Nautilus,* outmaneuvered destroyers with ease —as Momsen knew she would.

It took time, but the end was inevitable. Once battleship admirals fought a losing war to carrier advocates; now they in turn were being outflanked by submariners. The power plant of the *Nautilus* wedded to the *Albacore*'s hull would be an awesome weapon. And that, of course, was what happened. The main thrust of the Navy's nuclear effort went into the great, varied submarine fleet that it boasts today.

Before the marriage actually took place, Momsen would retire. He had put too many noses out of joint—just by being right, if nothing else. But with submariners in the ascendancy, he could let the new breed take over.

He was still on active duty, however, one wintry day in 1953 when he journeyed to the Portsmouth Navy Yard to deliver the commissioning address for the *Albacore,* that "ship and crew upon which so much depends." The podium he spoke from was especially appropriate; embedded in concrete as a permanent memorial to another day Swede Momsen had come to Portsmouth, it was part of the main deck and conning tower of the *Squalus.*

Decorations and Citations of
VICE ADMIRAL CHARLES BOWERS MOMSEN,
U.S. Navy

THE SECRETARY OF THE NAVY
WASHINGTON

9 MAY 1929

SIR:

The President of the United States takes pleasure in presenting the DISTINGUISHED SERVICE MEDAL to

LIEUTENANT CHARLES B. MOMSEN, U.S. NAVY

for service as set forth in the following

CITATION:

"For exceptionally meritorious and distinguished service to the government in the successful development of the escape device known as the 'lung.' During the early stages of its design and development Lieutenant Momsen, one of the inventors, courageously, repeatedly and voluntarily risked his life in conducting experiments of a nature such that there was little or no information available as to their probable results. In the later tests of the device when escapes were made from the U.S.S. S-4 submerged to depths as much as 207 feet Lieutenant Momsen was not only the first person to venture the escape but was also the leading and guiding spirit in all subsequent ones. It is through the initiative, courage and perseverance of Lieutenant Momsen that the development of the 'lung,' which has been pronounced as the greatest single contribution to Submarine Escape, has reached a successful conclusion and the device been adopted as part of the regular equipment of all our submarines."

For the President,
C. F. ADAMS
Secretary of the Navy

223

THE SECRETARY OF THE NAVY
WASHINGTON

The President of the United States takes pleasure in presenting the
LEGION OF MERIT to

REAR ADMIRAL CHARLES BOWERS MOMSEN

UNITED STATES NAVY

for service as set forth in the following

CITATION:

"For exceptionally meritorious conduct in the performance of outstanding services to the Government of the United States as Commander, Submarine Squadron Two of the United States Pacific Fleet,
during World War II. With unfailing patience and a careful analysis of the faulty performance of submarine torpedo exploders which
resulted in an alarming number of duds occurring in attacks by submarines of this force, Rear Admiral (then Captain) Momsen personally supervised an investigation to determine the weaknesses of
the exploder then in use and, correlating his own ideas with those
submitted by others, succeeded in developing a vastly improved
exploder which insured efficiency of our submarines in subsequent
actions. During one experimental phase of the program when a war
torpedo fired into a cliff failed to explode, he unhesitatingly, and at
great risk of life, entered the water and assisted in the recovery of
this live torpedo for further examination. By his professional skill,
untiring persistence and devotion to the fulfillment of an essential
mission, Rear Admiral Momsen contributed materially to the successful submarine warfare waged in the Pacific, thereby reflecting great
credit upon himself and the United States Naval Service."

For the President,
JAMES FORRESTAL
Secretary of the Navy

THE SECRETARY OF THE NAVY
WASHINGTON

The President of the United States takes pleasure in presenting the
NAVY CROSS to

REAR ADMIRAL CHARLES BOWERS MOMSEN

UNITED STATES NAVY

for service as set forth in the following

CITATION:

"For extraordinary heroism as Commander of a Coordinated
Attack Group of submarines operating in the enemy Japanese-
controlled waters of the East China Sea. A master of submarine warfare, Rear Admiral (then Captain) Momsen evolved a doctrine of
attack whereby submarines could be organized into an attack group
capable of operating deep in enemy-controlled waters while maintaining full striking power. As a result of his professional skill and
resolute leadership, the submarine under his command sank five
Japanese ships totaling over 38,000 tons and damaged eight ships
totaling over 63,000 tons. His devotion to duty reflects the highest
credit upon Rear Admiral Momsen and the United States Naval
Service."

For the President,
JAMES FORRESTAL
Secretary of the Navy

SUBMARINES PACIFIC FLEET

Be it known that

CAPTAIN C. B. MOMSEN

UNITED STATES NAVY

While Commanding THE FIRST SUBMARINE WOLFPACK has so distinguished himself by his Courage, Aggressiveness and Determination in action with the Enemy that his name has been inscribed on the

ROLL OF HONOR

of the

SUBMARINE BASE

C. E. ALDRICH
Captain U.S. Navy
Commander Submarine Base

Given this thirtieth
day of May, 1944, at the
Submarine Base
Pearl Harbor, T. of H.

THE SECRETARY OF THE NAVY
WASHINGTON

The President of the United States takes pleasure in presenting the GOLD STAR in lieu of the Second Legion of Merit to

REAR ADMIRAL CHARLES BOWERS MOMSEN
UNITED STATES NAVY

for service as set forth in the following

CITATION:

"For exceptionally meritorious conduct in the performance of outstanding services to the Government of the United States as Commander Submarine Squadron Two from February to November, 1943, and as Commander Submarine Squadron Four from November 1943 to May 1944, with additional duty as Chief of Staff, Commander Training Command, Submarine Force, United States Pacific Fleet, from November 1943 to April 1944. Through his excellent judgment and able supervision of the squadrons under his command, Rear Admiral (then Captain) Momsen was responsible in a large way for many war patrols in enemy waters, and in sinking many thousands of tons of hostile shipping skillfully and equitably discharging his duties as Chief of Staff, he contributed materially to the successful prosecution of submarine warfare in the Pacific area. His tireless devotion to duty was in keeping with the highest traditions of the United States Naval Service."

For the President,
JAMES FORRESTAL
Secretary of the Navy

COMMANDER FIFTH FLEET

The Commander FIFTH Fleet, United States Pacific Fleet, commends

CAPTAIN CHARLES BOWERS MOMSEN

UNITED STATES NAVY

for service as set forth in the following

CITATION:

"For meritorious conduct in the performance of his duties as Commanding Officer of the U.S.S. SOUTH DAKOTA in operations against the Japanese in support of the assault and occupation of Okinawa from 14 March to 14 May, 1945. Under his able command the U.S.S. SOUTH DAKOTA contributed materially to the damage inflicted upon the enemy and the protection afforded the fast carriers. His inspiring leadership and outstanding professional skill contributed to the success of the Okinawa operation. His conduct was at all times in keeping with the highest traditions of the United States Naval Service."

Commendation Ribbon authorized.

R. A. SPRUANCE
Admiral, U.S. Navy

THE SECRETARY OF THE NAVY

WASHINGTON

The President of the United States takes pleasure in presenting the GOLD STAR in lieu of the Third Legion of Merit to

REAR ADMIRAL CHARLES BOWERS MOMSEN

UNITED STATES NAVY

for service as set forth in the following

CITATION:

"For exceptionally meritorious conduct in the performance of outstanding services to the Government of the United States as Commanding Officer of the U.S.S. SOUTH DAKOTA, in action against enemy Japanese forces in the Pacific War Area from December 1944 to August 1945. Maintaining the fighting efficiency of his ship at a high level during prolonged and arduous combat operations, Rear Admiral (then Captain) Momsen contributed in a large measure to the infliction of serious damage upon enemy forces and shore installations and effectively directed his ship in numerous air actions and several bombardments of enemy shore defense including the first Naval bombardment of the Japanese main island of Honshu. His outstanding leadership was a material factor in keeping to a minimum the damage inflicted by the enemy on his Task Force, and his courage and devotion to duty were in keeping with the highest traditions of the United States Naval Service."

Rear Admiral Momsen is authorized to wear the Combat "V."

For the President,
JAMES FORRESTAL
Secretary of the Navy

THE SECRETARY OF WAR
WASHINGTON

The President of the United States takes pleasure in presenting the
DISTINGUISHED SERVICE MEDAL to

REAR ADMIRAL CHARLES B. MOMSEN

UNITED STATES NAVY

Rear Admiral Charles B. Momsen, United States Navy, performed exceptionally meritorious and distinguished service in Japan from November 1945 to October 1946. Serving as Administrator, Naval Shipping Control Authority for the Japanese Merchant Marine, United States Pacific Fleet, he directed the shipping of the Japanese Second Demobilization Bureau and the Japanese Civilian Merchant Marine in repatriating nearly six million people. He provided for the proficient training of Japanese crews, and resourcefully integrated United States and Japanese shipping into an effective organization which insured the safe and expeditious return of millions of displaced persons to their homes. Through his seasoned judgment, comprehensive knowledge and unremitting devotion to duty, Admiral Momsen contributed greatly to the fulfillment of occupational objectives.

For the President,
KENNETH C. ROYALL
Secretary of War

AUTHOR'S NOTE

I am indebted to the late Vice Admiral Momsen for his patience throughout the many days I spent interviewing him and for his ready response in all the correspondence that inevitably followed each session. In addition his own sense of history made my job a good deal easier than it otherwise would have been. This was especially true of the material afforded me by his scrupulously kept files of personal and official correspondence from the time he assumed command of the *S-1* in 1925 to his retirement in 1955, including such diverse papers as his plans for the first diving bell and the war diary of the first wolf pack patrol. Equally important in this regard were the journals he maintained, particularly from 1925 through 1939, and his numerous addresses and lectures, chief among them the "Rescue and Salvage of the U.S.S. *Squalus*" delivered before the Harvard Engineering Society, October 6, 1939; "Remarks at the Commissioning of the U.S.S. *Albacore*," December 5, 1935; and "Submarines Emerging from a 50-Year Dive" before the submarine officers of the Pacific Fleet, July 29, 1955.

The records of the U.S. Navy Submarine Safety Test Unit, 1929–32, were invaluable. So were the "Report on Use of Helium and Oxygen Mixtures" prepared by the experimental diving unit, April, 1939; "Medical Aspects of the Rescue and Salvage Operations of U.S.S. *Squalus* and the Use of Oxygen in Deep-Sea Diving," by Lieutenants A. R. Behnke and T. L. Willmon, *U.S. Naval Medical Bulletin*, October, 1939; the incredibly detailed, day-by-day, single-spaced typewritten progress report in three volumes totaling some 2,000 pages of the *Squalus Rescue and Salvage* forwarded to the Chief of Naval Operations by Rear Admiral Cole; and the *Log of Diving During Rescue and Salvage Operations of the U.S.S. Squalus* which precisely records the events of each trip of the rescue chamber and all six hundred and forty individual dives.

A number of those directly involved in the *Squalus* disaster are now dead; for others it was such a searing experience that even years later they still find it difficult to talk about. I would like to express my special thanks, however, to Rear Admiral Oliver F. Naquin, Mrs. Naquin and Mrs. Robert Greenlee for receiving me so graciously. In re-creating the events leading up to the dive of May 23rd and what subsequently happened on the bottom, I relied most heavily on Naquin's official report, the *Squalus* log during the crew's entombment, the written statements of all the *Squalus* survivors that were taken by the Navy immediately after their rescue and their subsequent oral testimony before the *Squalus* Court of Inquiry, which I was granted access to by the office of the Judge Advocate General, U.S. Navy. The remarks at the time of Harold C. Preble, Rear Admiral Cole, Captain R. S. Edwards, Commander A. I. McKee and Commander A. R. McCann were notably helpful.

Robert Trout of CBS was kind enough to give me both his recollections of the *Squalus* disaster and his broadcast transcripts; I was also enormously aided by the vivid reportage of the disaster itself, as well as the various stages of Momsen's career, by the Associated Press, the United Press, the *New York Times,* New York *Daily News,* the Washington *Post,* Washington *Star,* Washington *Times-Herald,* the Boston *Globe,* Boston *Herald,* Boston *Traveler,* Boston *Post* and the Portsmouth *Herald.*

For their comments on portions of the manuscript, I am most grateful to one of the Navy's great submariners, Captain Slade Cutter; master diver William Badders, who besides his courageous work during the *Squalus* rescue and salvage was with Momsen during the early days at Key West; and Hank Frey, Research Scientist in the Department of Oceanography and Meteorology, New York University. My thanks, finally, to Pat Sloatman and Marilyn Flaig for their assistance in preparing the manuscript, and to my editors, Evan Thomas and Ann Harris.

Any errors, needless to say, are mine.

PETER MAAS

BIBLIOGRAPHY

Barrows, Nathaniel A. *Blow All Ballast!* New York: Dodd, Mead, 1940.

Cousteau, Captain Jacques-Yves, with Frederic Dumas. *The Silent World.* New York: Harper, 1953.

Dugan, James. *Man Under the Sea.* New York: Harper, 1956.

Editors of *Navy Times. They Fought Under the Sea.* Harrisburg: Stackpole, 1962.

Ellsberg, Commander Edward, U.S.N. *On the Bottom.* New York: Dodd, Mead, 1929.

———. *Men Under the Sea.* New York: Dodd, Mead, 1939.

Frey, Hank and Shaney. *130 Feet Down.* New York: Harcourt, 1961.

Lockwood, Vice Admiral C. A., U.S.N. *Sink 'Em All.* New York: Dutton, 1951.

——— and Colonel Hans C. Adamson, U.S.A.F. *Hell at 50 Fathoms.* Philadelphia: Chilton, 1962.

Morison, Samuel Eliot. *History of United States Naval Operations in World War II,* Vol. VIII. Boston: Little, Brown, 1953.

Roscoe, Theodore. *United States Submarine Operations in World War II.* Annapolis: U.S. Naval Institute, 1949.

Shelford, Captain W. O., R.N. *Subsunk.* New York: Doubleday, 1960.

Warren, C. E. T., and James Benson. *Only Four Escaped.* New York: Sloane, 1959.

Periodicals

Momsen, Vice Admiral Charles B., with Peter Maas. "The Coming Death of the Surface Navy." *Look,* May 13, 1958.

Ryan, Cornelius. "I Rode the World's Fastest Sub." *Collier's,* April 1, 1955.

Smith, Beverly. "Russia's Submarines Are His Headache." *Saturday Evening Post,* May 28, 1949.

INDEX

About the Author

The Rescuer is Peter Maas's first full-length book, but he is widely known as the author of almost one hundred articles—profiles, muckraking exposés and political reportage—in such magazines as *Look, Esquire,* the *Saturday Evening Post, New York Magazine* and *Collier's.* Among his political profiles have been pieces on Robert Kennedy and Nelson Rockefeller. He wrote extensively about the Democratic campaign of 1960 and John Lindsay's mayoralty fight in 1965. His articles exposing Igor Cassini as a Trujillo agent, on Joseph Valachi and the Cosa Nostra, on charity fund raising and on children in jail attracted nationwide attention.

Mr. Maas was born in New York City in 1929 and grew up in Connecticut. He was educated at Duke University and the Sorbonne. After service in the Navy during the Korean War, he was on the staffs successively of *Collier's, Look* and the *Saturday Evening Post.* He lives in New York with his wife, novelist Audrey Gellen Maas, and their son John Michael, and devotes all his time to writing. He is now at work on his second book.

The idea for *The Rescuer* came to Mr. Maas as a result of his collaboration with Admiral Momsen on an article for *Look* called "The Coming Death of the Surface Navy." He worked on it intermittently for several years between other assignments, but the bulk of the writing was done during 1966.

Format by Katharine Sitterly
Set in Intertype Garamond
Composed, printed and bound by American Book–Stratford Press, Inc.
HARPER & ROW, PUBLISHERS, INCORPORATED